What the experts say about
BECOMING A MOTHER

". . . meets a real need in medical literature
for the layman. Highly recommended."

American Library Journal

*"Dr. Seidman is to be commended for giving a
great deal of authoritative information in a
very readable way . . . should prove a useful
and valuable book which many women in this
country would be glad to read."*

Medicine Illustrated
The British Journal of Clinical Practice

"An excellent book for obstetricians to recommend to their patients . . . easy and enjoyable reading."

Mississippi Valley Medical Journal

*"Anyone who has attempted a compendium
of obstetrics for the use of his own patients
will be impressed with this book. BECOMING
A MOTHER should prove a staunch ally to
the obstetrician who recommends it to his
patients."*

Karl F. Rugart, M.D.
Obstetrics and Gynecology

Becoming
a
Mother

by Theodore R. Seidman, M.D.

Committee on Obstetrics & Gynecology,
Doctors Hospital

and Marvin H. Albert

Revised Edition

FAWCETT CREST • NEW YORK

Copyright © 1956 by Theodore R. Seidman and Marion H. Albert

Published by Fawcett Crest Books, a unit of CBS Publications, the Educational and Professional Publishing Division of CBS, Inc. by arrangement with David McKay Company, Inc.

ISBN 0-449-20345-X

Printed in Canada

First Fawcett Crest Edition: August 1963

20   19   18   17   16

This book is dedicated
to ARLINE and MELBA,
to whom motherhood
is most becoming

CONTENTS

PART I: CONCEPTION

tion—The Rubin Test and X rays—Temperature charts, their use and abuse. *Some Causes of Infertility:* Blocked tubes—Cervical mucus unfavorable to sperm—Glandular disturbances—Abortions—Past illnesses—Age. *Misconceptions about Conception.* "Infantile" womb—Tipped womb—Hyperacidic vagina—Pre-control of a baby's sex. *Male Infertility:* A virile man is not necessarily a fertile man—Mechanical causes—Insufficient numbers of sperm—Poor-quality sperm—Frequency of intercourse and sperm quality—Artificial insemination with the husband's semen—Adoption versus artificial insemination with unknown donor. *Influence of Emotions on Fertility:* The emotional content of marriage—Sex practices that may interfere with conception—Nervous tension—Influence of the orgasm on conception —Does adoption help couples conceive?

Signs of Pregnancy: The first clues—Period-time staining after conception—False pregnancy. *Proof of Pregnancy:* Internal examination—Pregnancy tests.

PART II: PREGNANCY

How to Choose an Obstetrician: What kind of obstetrician?—"Painless" childbirth—"Natural" childbirth —Obstetrical fees—Compatibility. *Your First Visit to the Obstetrician:* Getting to know you—Your turn to ask questions. *Planning Your Hospitalization:* Choosing a hospital—Private or semi-private?—Delivery at home versus hospital—Rooming-in.

The Father's Role: His attitude is important. *Preparing for Fatherhood:* Education—Sharing the joy. *How He Can Help:* Understanding and encouragement—Easing the household work load—Love-making. *At the Hospital:* Separation and co-operation.

Contents

Becoming
a
Mother

PART I

Conception

Introduction

In ancient Babylon it was the custom to carry the sick to the market place, in the hope that some passer-by, familiar with the disease, might offer a helpful suggestion. Pregnancy has been called "a healthy sickness," but too often it is regarded as a sickness nevertheless. And for the pregnant woman the whole world is the market place, where everyone has a suggestion to make.

It is a tribute to the loyalty of woman that faith in her own doctor survives. His advice is so often contradicted by knowing friends quoting higher authority, or his words are reinterpreted for her until she is no longer sure what he said. The most trivial symptom is magnified into a warning of dread consequences. And even the absence of any complaint at all can evoke the doleful comment that "an easy beginning means a difficult end."

Anxiety begins before pregnancy—before there is any occasion to consult a physician. The miraculous discoveries that have exalted our faith in medical science seem to have diminished our faith in ourselves. The blessing of children was never taken for granted, but never before has tension mounted so rapidly in couples who want to conceive. To the old wives' tales of superstition have been added the young wives' tales of pseudo-science—overdramatization of the new and untried.

Only knowledge can dissipate doubt. Your obstetrician wants to be a teacher as well as a doctor. But women, though troubled, are afraid to reveal ignorance—or, seeing lines of fatigue on his face, are reluctant to take more of his time. He cannot provide answers to questions he does not hear. Even when asked, a casual manner may hide the underlying concern. To the doctor, a discharge from the navel means only a minor skin infection that will soon respond to treatment. He is astounded the first time he finds out that a woman's agitation over it is based on the fantastic conception that her own navel is directly connected to the baby.

No book can ever replace the guidance of your doctor. Nothing has been further from our minds than the creation of a sort of "do-it-yourself" manual for the economy-minded or for castaways on the traditional desert island. Self-diagnosis and self-treatment are poor medicine, even when you have a license to practice it.

Reading would not be helpful if it were likely to confuse you with statements too much opposed to those of your own doctor. The opinions of one obstetrician will not always coincide with those of another. But among the great majority, general agreement is much closer than you might be led to believe.

The voices of the few extremists are always heard. Common sense does not make bright conversation or sensational news stories. Neither can it approve those meddlesome practices that in slightly altered guise regain a vogue from time to time only to be discredited and forgotten.

This book actually represents a compilation of answers to the questions women ask day after day. To some the answers are very simple. All that is required is the assurance that the symptom is normal for that stage of pregnancy—just as a mother is satisfied when she finds that the behavior of her infant is normal for that stage of life. She does not need to know why.

Other questions involved rather detailed explanations. No matter how much she trusts her doctor, it is more difficult for a woman to carry out instructions unless she understands their purpose.

Every obstetrician recognizes that one of his most important functions is to calm the fears and promote the confidence of his patients. Yet this does not bar discussion of complications, since everyone knows that dangers exist—and a specific worry is better than a vague dread.

Childbirth can never be entirely without fear, even with all the statistics that prove its remarkable safety today. As man is never quite at home in the air despite millions of "passenger miles," neither can we hope to find in creation an element that can become natural or commonplace. Our aim can be only to relieve those nagging anxieties which degrade the spirit. The fear that remains is then more akin to awe, adding to the dignity of a human experience and to the love for those with whom we share it.

THEODORE R. SEIDMAN, M.D.

CHAPTER I

How You Become Pregnant

YOUR MENSTRUAL CYCLE

You were born to be a mother. When you entered this world, you brought with you the beginnings of the next generation. For when a baby girl is born, her tiny ovaries already contain about three hundred thousand eggs. All the eggs that she will ever have during her lifetime are already present at birth. You do not produce another single egg as long as you live—unlike a man, who produces his sperm as he goes along through his post-puberty life.

Of these approximately three hundred thousand eggs you will normally ripen only twelve each year—or less—during your menstrual life of about thirty years. In the course of your entire life as a menstruating woman no more than three hundred to three hundred fifty of the three hundred thousand eggs that you were born with will ripen and thus be capable of being fertilized.

It is believed that during a woman's childhood some development of eggs occasionally takes place. But these eggs never reach full maturity. Even the first few menstruations a girl experiences are not accompanied by egg ripening.

When the eggs that you were born with begin to ripen and leave your ovaries, you are ready to become a mother.

Ovulation. Ovulation is the maturing and freeing of a ripened egg by one of the two ovaries. This normally occurs once during each menstrual cycle—that is, about once a month.

There is a popular idea that a woman uses one ovary one month and the other ovary the next month. This is not true. A woman's ovaries do not alternate. The laws of chance dictate that if both ovaries are normal, a woman will use one

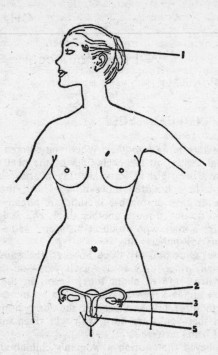

FIGURE A. The Organs of Conception

1. Pituitary gland
2. Fallopian tube
3. Ovary
4. Uterus (womb)
5. Cervix

about as often as the other, but not in alternating sequence. If you were tossing a coin, you wouldn't expect it to alternate, heads, then tails, then heads. You would expect to get perhaps three heads, then perhaps have it come up tails once or twice, then heads again. That is the way your ovaries work. Whichever ovary happens to respond first to the stimulus for the development of a mature egg is the one that produces the ripe egg that month.

Menstruation. A menstrual period (also referred to simply as a "period") is *normal* bleeding from the lining of the uterus (womb). The *onset* of menstrual bleeding marks the end of one menstrual cycle and the beginning of the next.

During your menstrual cycle a mature egg, ready to be fertilized by a male sperm, leaves one of your two ovaries. The egg travels through one of your two Fallopian tubes to your uterus. If you do not become pregnant (that is, if the egg is not fertilized), the egg passes through your uterus and out of your vagina, permitting a new cycle to follow.

During your menstrual cycle a new lining grows on the inner walls of your uterus to receive a fertilized egg. If the egg is not fertilized, and simply passes out through the uterus, the upper layers of the lining slough off. As the tissues break down, bleeding occurs. This is menstruation.

At one time it was believed that menstruation was proof that a woman was ovulating. This has been proved false. A woman may have a menstrual period even if she has not ovulated.

Your menstrual cycle. The interval between the start of one menstrual period and the start of the next period is known as your menstrual cycle. What happens to you during one typical cycle, if you do not become pregnant?

In the *first week* of your menstrual cycle, even while you are bleeding, your pituitary gland begins to stimulate the ripening of a new egg. The egg ripens in a blisterlike cyst (called a follicle) on the surface of one of your ovaries. As the egg follicle grows, it increases the amount of hormone secreted by the ovaries. This hormone acts upon the lining of the uterus, causing the glands to grow and the entire lining to thicken.

During the *second week* of your menstrual cycle the secretion of hormone by your ovaries becomes still stronger. This causes a clear mucus to pour from your cervix, which is the entrance to your uterus. Sperm can live for days in this type of cervical mucus. At the end of the second week the egg follicle bursts, setting free the ripe egg from your ovary. This ripening and setting free of the mature egg is ovulation.

During the *third week* the ripe egg travels down one of your Fallopian tubes (which serve as pathways from the ovaries to the uterus). Another ovarian hormone is now at work causing special changes in the lining of your uterus which prepare it for receiving a fertilized egg. At the end of

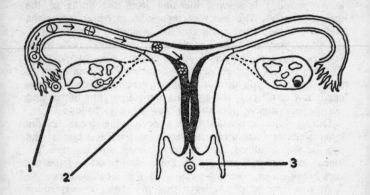

FIGURE B. Travel of a Ripe Egg

1. Ripened egg is extruded from the surface of the ovary and enters the Fallopian tube. It is here that the egg is normally impregnated by sperm swarming toward it through the tube.
2. After traveling through the tube and entering the uterus, the egg, if it has been fertilized by a sperm, implants itself in the lining of the uterus, and pregnancy begins.
3. If the egg is not fertilized, it disintegrates during its travel through the tube and uterus, passing out of the uterus.

the third week, the egg, having traversed the Fallopian tube, enters the uterus. Since the egg was not fertilized, it has been distintegrating in its passage through the tube and into the uterus. During this week in the cycle, also, the cervical mucus becomes thick, and sperm no longer thrive in it.

In the *fourth week* of your menstrual cycle, when the egg has not been fertilized, the egg follicle on the ovary shrinks. The output of the second ovarian hormone then ceases. The absence of this hormone causes the vessels supplying the thickened lining of your uterus to go into spasm and bleed. With the bleeding, about two thirds of the tissue lining the walls of your uterus sloughs away. This is your menstrual period. One menstrual cycle has now been completed; a new cycle is starting.

WHEN PREGNANCY OCCURS

Conception. What happens to your menstrual cycle when conception occurs? To understand this, you must first know *how* conception takes place.

Conception occurs shortly after the egg is ejected from your ovary. It takes place in the upper end of one of your Fallopian tubes, close to one of your ovaries. There are such things as ovarian pregnancies, where apparently the egg was fertilized right in the ovary. But this is so rare as to constitute a medical curiosity.

Usually, conception happens in this way:

When sperm leave the male, they are ejaculated into the vagina of the woman. The ejaculation (semen) amounts to about a teaspoonful of fluid. Part of this fluid escapes from the vagina immediately. But since the average ejaculate contains millions of sperm, if only a third of it is retained there are still plenty of sperm to do the job.

The purpose of this relatively large volume of semen is temporarily to neutralize the normally acid vaginal secretions. These secretions will kill any sperm that remain in the vagina too long. The fluid in which the sperm is ejaculated from the male serves as temporary protection. But unless the sperm succeeds in escaping upward from the vagina—through the cervix, into the uterus and Fallopian tubes—the sperm will be killed by the acid vaginal secretions in an hour or two.

At a favorable time of the month there is an outpouring of a clear mucus from your cervix. Once the sperm escapes from the vagina, into this mucus, it can live anywhere from two to five days. The whole genital canal, from the cervix upward, becomes a reservoir of living, wriggling sperm. It is because of this that intercourse need not take place on the same day that ovulation occurs for you to become pregnant. The sperm may be present and waiting for two or three days before the ripened egg leaves the ovary.

No one knows exactly how long sperm can survive in this cervical mucus and still retain the ability to fertilize an egg. But *after* the egg is ejected from the ovary, it must be fertilized within eight to twelve hours or it begins to disintegrate and is no longer capable of reproduction.

When the egg leaves the ovary, it flows into the Fallopian

tube. It is met almost immediately by a swarm of sperm ascending from the cervical mucus.

It may be assumed that the egg will be fertilized by a sperm that has come up through the tube that is nearer. However, if the tube is blocked, the egg may sometimes be fertilized by sperm from the opposite tube. Usually the egg will migrate into the tube on its own side. But there are cases of transmigration of the egg, where it migrates to the tube on the other side.

If one sperm succeeds in penetrating and fertilizing the ripe egg, no other sperm can enter the egg. Conception has taken place.

But when this happens, you are still not pregnant. The fertilized egg is still in no way attached to you. You will not be pregnant until the fertilized egg multiplies into a cluster of cells, forming a tiny ball, and implants itself in the wall of the uterus. This happens about seven days after conception.

How conception alters your menstrual cycle. When conception occurs, the fertilized egg takes about a week to descend through your Fallopian tube and begin to implant in the inner wall of the uterus. During its seven days of travel through the tube (which is only three-and-a-half inches long), the fertilized egg undergoes many cell divisions, forming a cluster of cells called an ovum. This ovum arrives in the uterus on about the twenty-first day of your menstrual cycle.

The ovum burrows into the lining of the uterus, implants itself there, and proceeds to grow. This is actually the beginning of pregnancy, but you would still have no way of knowing what is happening inside you.

When the ovum attaches to the uterus, it produces an effect upon the pituitary gland that causes the level of hormone secretion to remain high. Because of this continuing hormone action, the thickened lining of the uterus does not slough away as it does when the hormone secretion drops. Instead, the lining of the uterus continues to thrive. No period occurs, and you first begin to suspect that you have become pregnant.

Tubal pregnancies. A fertilized egg must spend seven days traversing the distance from the ovary, through the Fallopian tube, into the uterus. If the descent of the egg through the tube is too rapid, it reaches the uterus before it has become sufficiently developed to attach itself to the lining of the uterus. It passes out unrecognized in the vaginal discharges.

If the passage of the egg through the tube is too slow, on the other hand, the egg reaches the stage of development where it requires nourishment from the uterus lining before it has reached the uterus. If this happens, the fertilized egg usually dies and disintegrates. But in some cases, instead of disintegrating, the egg implants itself in the wall of the tube, and begins to grow there. This is a tubal pregnancy, which eventually bursts the tube. It calls for an emergency operation.

There have been too many horror stories about tubal pregnancies. In the days before blood banks, mortality was high. But now that blood can be replaced quickly, the danger is small if the woman is in the hands of a doctor. The tubal pregnancy usually does not just develop and rupture without first giving signs that will warn the doctor to be on the alert.

The only thing that should be stressed about the possibility of tubal pregnancy is that you should see a doctor as soon as staining or any abdominal discomfort appears after you miss a period. Tubal pregnancies are not common. But too often a woman assumes that such staining can only mean a possible miscarriage, and defers going to a doctor because she is afraid that internal examination will make it more likely. Not only is such fear groundless, but it may lead to catastrophe by delaying the detection of this condition until serious internal bleeding occurs.

Some women are afraid that they will not be able to conceive again after a tubal pregnancy operation. This is not true. A tubal pregnancy involves only one of the two Fallopian tubes. Because of the emergency nature of the operation, and the fact that there is little likelihood of a second tubal pregnancy, the surgeon will usually remove the tube that contains the pregnancy. The woman still has her other tube, and can have a normal pregnancy the next time.

Twins. You will have identical twins if this happens shortly after you conceive: Your egg, which has been fertilized by a single sperm, goes through several cell divisions, and then the cluster of cells that form the resulting ovum splits into two separate parts. Each of these two parts grows into a complete individual, and you give birth to twins who look alike and are of the same sex. If one of the two parts splits again shortly after the first separation, you have identical triplets.

The tendency to identical twins can be inherited through either the husband's sperm or the wife's egg. But only the wife can take the credit—or the blame—for non-identical twins. It happens in this way: If you ripen two eggs that are extruded from your ovaries in the same menstrual cycle, each may be separately fertilized—and you have non-identical twins. Since the twins in this case are formed by two different eggs fertilized by two different sperm, they will be as different from each other as brothers and sisters who are not twins. These are known as fraternal twins.

"FERTILE" AND "SAFE" PERIODS

The "fertile period." The time during each menstrual cycle in which intercourse is likely to result in pregnancy is called the "fertile period." It is determined by when you ovulate. Just how long your fertile period lasts depends on how long sperm can survive inside you, waiting for you to ovulate. You can become pregnant if you have had intercourse one, two, or perhaps even five days before ovulation. But once you do ovulate, your fertile period ends within a few hours. You can no longer conceive during the rest of the month—unless intercourse takes places within a very few hours after ovulation.

This fertile time differs in each woman. But you can usually calculate *about* when your own fertile period occurs by referring to when your next period is expected. If an egg is not fertilized, menstruation occurs about two weeks after ovulation. In other words, you ovulate about fourteen days *before* a period. So you could usually assume that you were having your fertile period sometime during twelve to sixteen days *before your next* menstrual period. The common error is to assume that the fertile period for all women is a certain number of days *after* a period.

If a woman has a cycle of twenty-five days from the onset of one menstrual bleeding to the onset of the next bleeding, her ovulations could take place about eleven days after the beginning of a period. That would be fourteen days before her next period was expected.

A woman whose cycle from onset to onset of bleeding is thirty-five days could be expected to ovulate about twenty-one days after the start of a period. This would still be fourteen days before the next period. The fertile time in this woman, therefore, would be about ten days later than in the first woman.

But in calculating your fertile period, you should remember that you might be right about it one month and wrong the next. If your time of ovulation varies, the fertile period will vary with it. Some women have very irregular cycles, with ovulation occurring at different times in different months. And there is also the possibility that ovulation may be hastened or retarded by emotional factors. In rabbits, cats, and ferrets, sexual excitement brings on ovulation. We have no proof that this happens in a human. But it is distinctly possible.

The "safe period." The other side of the coin from the fertile period is what is often referred to as the "safe period." This is the time during a menstrual cycle in which intercourse is unlikely to result in pregnancy. Ordinarily, if intercourse took place more than four or five days before ovulation, or more than twelve hours after ovulation, no pregnancy could result. But the "safe period" quite often becomes "unsafe." There is always the chance of inaccuracy in determining when you ovulate. And, as was pointed out in the previous section, the time of ovulation can shift, either because the menstrual cycle is irregular, or because of the possibility that ovulation can be stimulated out of season by strong sexual emotions.

Can you conceive during a period? In a woman with a relatively short menstrual cycle, ovulation may take place as early as seven days after a menstrual period begins. If this woman has a long menstrual period, she might still be staining when ovulation took place. In such a case, she could conceive while she appeared to still to be having her period.

From this you can see that the time close to the end of a period, which is usually relatively "safe," may actually be some women's fertile time. A woman can also become pregnant during the other usually "safe" time: just *before* an expected period. This is because you never know how close an expected period really is. A period may be delayed a week for causes unknown, and emotional factors may so stimulate ovulation that it occurs at just this time.

Birth control pills. During the past few years birth control pills have received extensive tests. These are progesterone-like compounds such as are used to prevent miscarriage. They act by suppressing the pituitary gland so that it does not stimulate the ovary to release eggs.

To prevent conception a pill is taken every day for 20

days, starting on the fifth day of menstruation. This is early enough to prevent ovulation. The compound builds up the lining of the uterus as though ovulation had taken place. When the medication is stopped on the twentieth day, the lining breaks down and begins to bleed about two days later, thus creating an artificial menstrual cycle.

The effectiveness of this medication is well established. Its known side effects include pregnancy-like symptoms, nausea, sensitive breasts and a type of staining called "break-through bleeding."

CHAPTER 2

Questions Women Ask About Themselves

About this chapter. Before pregnancy, even long before marriage, awareness of the fact that she is a potential mother is part of a woman's mind and emotions. Having babies becomes a concern to young girls at an amazingly early age while marriage itself is still but half a daydream. Much of the worry over menstruation, feminine hygiene, sex practices, illnesses, or operations, stems from fear of possible effect on the reproductive organs and future childbearing. This chapter is devoted to answering the questions on these subjects that are asked of me by mothers, mothers-to-be, and would-be mothers.

MENSTRUATION

At what age should menstruation start? Most girls begin to menstruate during their thirteenth year of life. But it may start—in perfectly healthy girls—as early as the eleventh year, or as late as the seventeenth. Climate and race appear to have very little influence.

If a girl begins to menstruate before the age of ten, it is wise to have her examined, to rule out the possibility of a glandular tumor causing precocious puberty. A delay in the appearance of menstruation beyond sixteen years warrants thorough investigation to rule out factors that may tend to obstruct the flow or retard sexual development.

How regular should menstruation be? A girl may be very irregular. There is no cause for alarm if she menstruates once or twice and then skips a whole year. Most people understand this. But mothers of adolescent girls are frequently impatient for the appearance of more regular and heavier menstrual bleeding because they think that this will improve their daughters' health and disposition.

It is perfectly true that malnutrition, emotional tension, or poor health may suppress menstruation for long periods of time. In the Nazi concentration camps a combination of all three factors was at work. Disappearance of menstruation during confinement was such a common experience that young women who survived it assumed that the Nazis had been administering some special drug for that purpose. Even where health and food conditions are good, emotional factors alone may have a similar effect. It is not an uncommon occurrence with student nurses first entering training.

Excitement may also produce the opposite reaction, bringing on a menstrual period before it is expected, as many a bride has learned to her embarrassment.

But while it is true that poor health, mental or physical, may cause menstrual irregularity, it is not true that regular menstruation is necessary for good health or will bring it about.

The notion that the menstrual flow represents some poisonous element extracted from the blood is widely believed. Medical experience indicates that it is not true. A woman with infrequent periods may remain in the best of health. And a woman who has too much menstrual bleeding may find her health vastly improved by hysterectomy, which allows her to retain her blood, "poisons" and all.

For the average woman, twenty-four to thirty-one days elapse from the beginning of one menstrual period to the beginning of the next. Most women are not regular as clockwork. They show a variation of at least two or three days one way or the other. This variation is likely to grow much greater in the middle years, before menstruation ceases entirely.

Following a pregnancy, there is a brief phase of menstrual irregularity frequently responsible for needless alarm. And women who nurse their infants may find their periods scanty or entirely suppressed. Marriage itself may cause remarkable changes in the menstrual cycle.

But despite the wide range and variations in normal menstruation there are limits beyond which it can be considered abnormal, reason to seek medical advice.

If your menstrual cycle—from onset to onset of bleeding—is regularly less than twenty-one days, it probably indicates glandular imbalance and failure of ovulation. Hormone treatment can sometimes correct this.

If menstrual periods are too profuse or last too long, your health will suffer because you are not able to regenerate quickly enough the amount of blood that you lose each month. The maximum length of time that a normal period lasts is about eight days. If periods last longer than that, it is definitely abnormal, and you should consult a gynecologist in order to correct the condition. It can happen once or twice, however, with no definite cause to be found and no treatment required.

Periods that are too scanty or infrequent also require medical attention. It can be considered an abnormal sign if you have very little bleeding during a period, if your period lasts less than two days, or if your menstrual cycle—from the start of one period to the start of the next—is longer than five weeks. In some cases, however, it will be found that no treatment is required.

Any woman past the age of sixteen, whose periods have been well established, should certainly see a doctor if her periods become suppressed. This can happen at any time during adult life because of emotional factors, as was pointed out before, and no treatment be required. But if it is accompanied by other bodily changes—in weight, quantity and distribution of body hair, voice, breast development—it requires careful study.

Painful menstruation is not uncommon. If it is what is known medically as primary dysmenorrhea—where menstruation was painful from its very start—it is not an indication of organic disease. But acquired dysmenorrhea—when menstruation for some years was perfectly normal, and then became increasingly painful—may be a danger sign. A doctor should be consulted about it.

Any fundamental change in the pattern of your periods or menstrual cycle is reason to consult a doctor.

How much activity is permissible during a period? There are physical culturalists who insist that women should take rather strenuous exercise during periods, in the belief that this will cure menstrual cramps and all other ills associated with periods. While this is an exaggerated view, it is true that for a normal woman there is no physical reason to curtail activities during a period. This includes sports.

Taking a bath, a shower, or a swim during a period is also permissible. There *is* a reflex effect on blood flow in the pelvis that may take place on immersing the body in water, causing a temporary cessation of menstruation. But this does no harm. It does not cause any disturbances in the menstrual cycle.

Many women, of course, do not feel physically at par during their periods. There is no reason why they should not take it easy until they feel better. But if a woman feels fine, there is no restriction on the amount of physical activity in which she may indulge.

Sexual intercourse during the menstrual period is subject to religious taboo and generally considered distasteful. But it is frequently practiced and no harmful result has been observed.

Is internal protection during periods safe? I know of no instance where any serious harm has been caused by the use of internal protection—tampons such as Tampax, Meds, Fibs, etc.—during periods.

When vaginal secretions are kept inside the body, saturating a sterile piece of material, it does have a tendency to become foul, indicating that there is a growth of bacteria. Vaginal secretions differ in different women. Some women have more of a tendency than others to harbor the kind of bacteria that can produce offensive odors. Therefore, internal protection should be used, first of all, only by women who notice in themselves no tendency to develop irritating discharges or offensive odors. It should be changed every few hours. And it should be removed with sufficient attention to make sure that none of it is left inside.

Is staining between periods dangerous? Any type of bleeding or staining at irregular intervals between periods merits investigation. Its cause need not be anything serious, but only a doctor can decide.

It is not unusual for a woman to notice a slight staining—either pinkish or brownish—almost exactly in the middle of her menstrual cycle, around the time of ovulation. This simply may be "ovulation bleeding," which requires no treatment. However, it should be checked first by a physician before it can be safely ignored.

If you stain after intercourse you should see a doctor. It is not necessarily dangerous; there are many harmless conditions that can cause it. But only a physician can determine whether it is harmless or not.

Staining may occur, quite normally, just before a period gets fully started, and may continue for varying intervals after a period is over. It does not usually require any medical investigation, unless it represents a definite change for you. As with any other sudden change in body function, it calls for a checkup.

Are vaginal discharges a danger sign? Women, even from infancy, can have discharges from the vagina. It is quite a problem with a little girl, and whether the vaginal discharge is profuse or slight, she should be taken to the doctor for at least one examination. However, if the first examination does not disclose any serious infection, and if no foreign body or growth is found in the vagina, it is unwise to concentrate too much effort on trying to cure the condition. Frequent examinations and treatments are very distressing to a child and may have psychological effects that are more serious than the local condition.

In the adolescent girl, particularly under moments of stress —school examinations, competitions, romances, the typical mother-daughter hostility—there is very apt to be an oversecretion by the glands of the cervix (the entrance of the womb). This organ is under the control of the sympathetic nervous system which also controls the rate of the heartbeat and the rate of peristaltic movement of the intestines. The vaginal discharge resulting from such oversecretion is simply a nervous manifestation, rather than an infection.

At any age, with or without sexual contact, it is possible for a woman to develop infections of the lining of the vagina which, while not serious, can be quite annoying. One of these conditions, which is becoming more and more common today, is infection with a type of fungus. This fungus is commonly found in the vagina, even in women having no symptoms. It occasionally infects the mouths of newborn infants with a condition known as thrush. Fungus infections of the vagina are more common today because of the wider use of antibiotics. The antibiotics, although they cure diseases, frequently have the effect of upsetting the balance of nature. The fungi that lie harmlessly in the vagina are not at all affected by the antibiotics in common use. When antibiotics kill off the competing organisms living in the vagina, the fungi find their growth unopposed. They then grow to such an extent that they cause severe irritation and a thick yellowish discharge.

This condition, like many other types of vaginal infection, is apt to flare up after menstrual periods. Menstrual blood appears to act as a culture media, giving the offending organisms a start toward a growth that can end by producing vaginal infections. It is for this reason that I suggested earlier that women finding themselves prone to vaginal infections avoid using internal protection during periods. Any material kept in the vagina becomes saturated with blood that, being maintained at body temperature, promotes the growth of certain types of bacteria.

Another type of vaginal discharge that is not uncommon in the unmarried as well as the married woman, in virgin as well as mother, is due to a microscopic animal parasite known as trichomonas vaginalis. This organism is probably the most frequent cause of itching and irritating vaginal discharges. It can occur at any age. The type of discharge associated with it is much thinner than that associated with the fungus infection, but the itching is just as intense.

There are many medications that are successful in treating either of these two vaginal infections. No serious harm can result from either one of them. However, they may prove quite stubborn and require frequent treatment before they are finally eradicated. Recurrence after a year or more is not uncommon.

DOUCHING

Should a woman douche? It is wrong to argue either that no woman should douche or that all women should douche. The woman who needs to, should douche.

The type of vaginal secretion varies in different women. Normal women are fortunate enough to have a slightly acid vaginal secretion that kills off bacteria which tend to putrefy and cause unpleasant odors. Such women never need to use a douche. Other women have a type of vaginal secretion that allows bacteria to grow and cause unpleasant odors.

No woman needs to douche more than once or twice a week—except for special treatment under a doctor's orders. If a woman feels she must douche more often, she is either suffering from some local condition that requires treatment by a doctor, or else she is suffering from one of the neuroses of our age, which considers all human odors objectionable.

It is wise for any woman who has never douched before, or who has any doubts about the proper method, to ask her doctor about it. The correct method is simple, and can cause no harm.

What should be used as a douche? The main function of a douche—as used by a woman without a doctor's orders—is simply a mechanical flushing action to remove a discharge or the last traces of blood from a menstrual period that may form the material upon which offensive bacteria grow.

At one time it was popular to use alkaline solutions whose main ingredient was bicarbonate of soda. The theory popular at the time was the erroneous one that everything acid was unhealthy and anything alkaline was healthy. Since vaginal secretions are acid, the idea was to flush them away with bicarbonate of soda in an effort to make them alkaline. This, under normal conditions, did not succeed, because Nature is very stubborn about how she has ordered things.

Then some thoughtful doctor decided that vaginal secretions were acid because they were meant to be. It was decided that vinegar, being a handy and harmless weak acid present in every household, would, when diluted, serve as a good douche, since it would not interfere with the normal acidity of vaginal secretions. But since vinegar is neither fragrant, nor antiseptic, nor detergent, it can accomplish nothing therapeutic in the concentration in which it is likely to be used.

No douche can possibly sterilize the vagina, even if it were desirable. No douche can materially affect the type of bacteria growing in the vagina. The most a douche can do is, by cleansing, temporarily to eliminate offensive odors. Therefore, antiseptics and irritating chemicals should not be used. The most useful douche is one that has a mild detergent action and is pleasantly fragrant. Such douches are commercially available in any drugstore. Look at the label. The typical ingredients of a mild douche powder would consist of: sodium chloride, boric acid, sodium lauryl sulphate—with essential oils such as thymol, or eucalyptol for fragrance. Some douches contain alum or zinc chloride for mild astringent effect.

AGE

When should a woman consider herself too old for pregnancy? One of the matters of greatest concern to women is the question of whether they are too old to have a baby. It has been traditional among obstetricians to refer to women pregnant *for the first time* after thirty-five as elderly. It is true that in the older groups, from thirty-five to forty, there is an increased occurrence of high blood pressure which may be aggravated during pregnancy. There is also the greater likelihood, the older a woman is, that she has acquired one of the chronic diseases. But if a woman is in good health and able to conceive, she will usually encounter no special difficulty in carrying a child through pregnancy—whether she is thirty-five or forty-five.

As far as labor is concerned, if a woman's bone structure is normal there is no reason not to allow her to enter labor in hope of a normal birth, regardless of her age. In some cases, it is true, the uterine contractions function less efficiently as a woman gets older. The cervix, that portion of the uterus which must dilate in labor, appears less elastic. In such cases, because there is not too great a likelihood of future pregnancies, most obstetricians would—in case of doubt—feel it was better to resort to a Caesarean section.

In my own experience, women up to the age of forty-seven have had first babies without unusual difficulty.

MENOPAUSE

What is menopause? Menopause, the so-called "change of life," is the cessation of ovulation and menstruation. There are two kinds of menopause. First, there is the natural menopause which every woman can expect when her childbearing days are over. The other kind is surgical or radiation menopause, where a doctor either removes the uterus, ovaries, or both, or destroys their function with X rays or radium when disease makes such treatment necessary. Surgical menopause has no relation to a woman's age.

When can you expect menopause? There is a common misconception that women who start menstruating late reach the menopause later. This belief probably stems from our instinctive sense of fair play—the feeling that all women ought to have the same number of childbearing years allotted to them.

But the truth is quite the opposite: A girl who starts menstruating at ten or eleven may continue into her fifties. A girl who starts at seventeen is likely to terminate in her early forties or even her late thirties. The later a girl begins to menstruate, the earlier she will normally reach menopause.

Menopause occurs in this country generally sometime in the middle forties. But it may occur as early as the middle thirties or as late as the late fifties.

How does menopause begin? Ovulation and menstruation do not terminate simultaneously. As a woman grows older, she may ovulate less and less often, even though menstrual periods continue to be fairly regular.

Sooner or later a woman skips a period because menopause has begun. But since the skipping of a period is also usually the first sign that a woman has conceived, she may think she had become pregnant. A pregnancy test at this time may show, *falsely,* that she *is* pregnant. In some cases a woman is so unnerved at the prospect of having a baby at this late stage in life that she will do silly—and dangerous—things.

Most pregnancy tests are based on the reaction of test animals to increased amounts of pituitary hormone in the urine of a pregnant woman. After menopause begins, a woman's ovarian secretions become weaker. And the weaker they become, the stronger her pituitary secretion grows, in what may be described as an attempt to stir up more activity on the part of the ovary. There may be enough spilling over of this extra pituitary secretion into the urine to give a false positive test and make a woman believe she is pregnant when she is not.

Other women may err in the opposite direction. Sometimes during menopause a woman will stop taking precautions against pregnancy as soon as her periods stop—thinking them no longer necessary. She may find herself pregnant if she does this—despite the fact that months have gone by without a period. For many a woman has stopped menstruating for six months or a year—and then had another period or two. There is no way of knowing whether or not ovulation has preceded these periods.

Will menopause harm your health and looks? Menopause should require very little treatment. It is a normal stage of life, not a disaster requiring emergency-rescue techniques.

The most common fears that women harbor about menopause are that they will lose their feminine attractiveness, that hair will grow in unsightly places, that their sex desires will vanish, that a great many mental and physical troubles will begin. None of these things need follow. We must face the fact that the bloom of youth cannot last forever. But the woman who happens to have an early menopause does not, as a result, age earlier.

Many of the problems associated with menopause are psychological. But these psychological troubles, also, are not caused in any great measure by menopause itself. In most cases, such nervous symptoms are only coincidentally connected with changes in menstrual life. These symptoms occur at that time simply because menopause usually happens at an age when the stresses of life seem to crowd about one.

At this time, because you have older relatives and friends, serious illness and death seem to strike more closely. Also, a woman who has grown to regard herself essentially as a mother with children to care for and discipline suddenly finds herself out of a job. Her children are teen-agers or older. They require less and less of her attention. Hostility frequently arises between a mother and her adolescent daughter.

It is true, however, that changes in the amount of circulating hormones, if sudden and vast enough, can cause changes in a person's mood. The same thing happens after childbirth: The large quantity of hormone that circulates in the blood of a pregnant woman suddenly drops to the low pre-pregnancy level. This sudden drop in the amount of circulating hormones certainly contributes to the period of depression that frequently follows birth. Similarly, there may be depression because of the changing level of circulating hormones during menopause. But, as with post-pregnancy depression, those women who exhibit extreme emotional disturbance at this time have usually had emotional difficulties at other stages of their lives.

The normal degree of moodiness and the sudden waves of heat and perspiration that sometimes accompany these hormone changes can often be relieved by the use of sufficient amounts of estrogen. Extreme emotional disturbance is usually not helped by the administration of any amount of hormone, indicating that such disturbance is not caused by menopause itself, but by some underlying psychic problem.

CHAPTER 3

Medical Help for Infertility

WHEN TO SEE A DOCTOR

You want to have a baby. For most couples who decide it is time to have a baby, the next step is easy. For others the path to parenthood is beset with difficulty.

It may appear that more couples are having difficulty conceiving in these tense and troubled times. The problem of fertility and infertility seems to be distressing this generation more than those of the past. But it only seems this way. Religious customs that go back beyond recorded history, the most ancient literature, including the Bible, all give evidence that fertility has ever been an important problem for the human race. Primitive and advanced societies alike have recognized that children are a blessing that is not always forthcoming.

Every religion of the past has had rites to encourage the favor of the gods in promoting conception and childbirth. Every tribe has had its charms and incantations aimed at bringing about this favorable issue for those to whom children did not come quickly and automatically. But today, living in an age of unparalleled faith in medical science, couples are more likely to turn to their physician for aid.

When do you need medical help? How long should you try to become pregnant before failure warrants seeing a doctor about it? To the question of how quickly pregnancy should occur there is no exact answer in number of months. Many couples conceive the first month they try. But it is not unusual for otherwise normal couples to try for a full year before pregnancy is achieved.

If a couple has tried to have a baby for a year without success, it is time for them to see a doctor. The wife will be given a complete gynecological examination and her husband's fertility will also be investigated thoroughly.

But if a couple are worried about their failure to conceive —even if they have been trying for less than a year—they should not wait before consulting a physician. Whenever failure to conceive becomes a worry to a couple, and thus a problem in their marriage, they need medical help. Although a full sterility investigation may not be warranted, an examination and a talk with the doctor may be reassuring.

If they did not have a general physical examination before marriage, it is a good idea for a couple to have one at some time in early marriage before they begin planning to have children. This preliminary visit to the doctor should be limited to a general physical and gynecological examination. One purpose of this examination is to make sure that there is no *obvious* abnormality that will interfere with conception.

Of course, some couples do have more reason than others to worry about the possibility of infertility. The young woman who has had a great deal of menstrual difficulty, who has had operations on her pelvic organs, who has had a ruptured appendix or other type of peritonitis, has more reason to be anxious. Men may suspect some interference with their fertility if during adolescence they acquired mumps with involvement of both testicles. In such cases, it is probably wise to consult a doctor earlier to determine if there is a fertility problem.

Some couples worry about whether they *should* try to have children. Women who have had heart disease, kidney disease, diabetes, tuberculosis, or epilepsy have reason to be concerned about the wisdom of undertaking pregnancy. The effect of these diseases on pregnancy is discussed completely in Chapter 9, in the part of this book that deals with pregnancy. Whether or not you should contemplate pregnancy if you have one of these diseases depends in large measure on the current condition of the disease, and only a doctor can advise you on this. In a majority of cases pregnancy may be undertaken with little or no extra risk, although in some cases you may require special care.

THE DOCTOR VERSUS INFERTILITY

Every sterility case is an individual problem. I don't believe that anyone working in the field of infertility can honestly be sure of the number of couples he has helped to have children. This does not mean that sterility is a hopeless condition. On the contrary, 75 per cent of the couples who go to doctors because of infertility eventually do have children. But what percentage of them would have had children anyway it is very hard to say.

This is the unfortunate part of sterility work. From the most ancient times, people have been quick to give credit to whatever they did just before they became pregnant. A reputation for "sterility miracles" comes easily. A woman who has been trying to become pregnant for years sees many doctors. Finally she does become pregnant. Immediately the word goes out through everyone she knows that her latest doctor is the man who cures sterility. Women who have been trying to get pregnant for ten years, who have been going to the best men in the field, will suddenly appear in his office—convinced that he has some special genius or knows something that a dozen other doctors don't.

Conception remains a mystery. It is a very complicated process. There are so many points at which it can go wrong. Our methods of investigation are still very inexact. It is like having carpenters' tools to repair a fine watch. We can't actually see a great many of the processes involved. We have no way at the present time of determining whether the mechanism that controls the rate at which the fertilized egg descends into the uterus is functioning properly or not. We can only determine that the tubes present an open passage and appear normal anatomically. Sperm we can judge only by their appearance and activity. Yet we know that the sperm of one species may look the same as that of another, yet can fertilize only its own kind.

There can be no routine for treatment of infertility—beyond a few preliminary tests for quality of semen, condition of tubes, ability of cervical mucus to maintain the life of the sperm, and evidence as to whether an egg is ripened. After these tests are performed, each sterility case becomes a research problem of its own. Each is a mystery and a challenge, and must be treated as an experiment.

After a couple have been given the preliminary tests, if no obvious abnormality has been discovered, the doctor will try different approaches to their problem. If one approach does not work, another is tried. Always it is trial and error.

Even when the couple finally succeed in conceiving, the doctor seldom knows how much he has helped. If a doctor surgically corrects an abnormality, he can feel solely responsible for curing sterility. But there are few other types of treatment where he can be certain of his part in subsequent conception. Many a couple have remained infertile for years, for no obvious cause, and then suddenly achieved fertility for causes still obscure.

Modesty is called for on the part of any doctor dealing with infertility at the present time. He never knows how many victories he has a right to claim as his own—and how many times he merely encouraged people to be patient while nature did the rest. This is an area of human experience before which a doctor feels humble. Many so-called advances, once hailed as sensational, have since proved of little value. We are only on the threshold of a science that can understand the chemistry of genetics and heredity.

Absolute sterility and relative infertility. There are only a few specific things that doctors can do to overcome obstacles which would absolutely prevent pregnancy. An example of one of these few things would be the case of a woman whose tubes have been sealed by disease. She could conceive only if she were operated on successfully and her tubes opened. In such circumstances, the gynecologist could claim full credit for having made fertile a woman who could never have conceived before.

But aside from such correction of anatomical defects, it is doubtful whether medical treatment can convert a couple who are absolutely sterile into a couple who can from then on conceive with normal ease.

Most problems are fortunately not in this absolute-sterility category but involve a relative infertility—a matter of *degree* of fertility or infertility. The lower the fertility in a couple, the less chance they have of conceiving. But that does not mean that they cannot or will not conceive.

It is as though the wife with her eggs represents the prizes in a lottery. The more fertile the wife is—the more favorable the environment she provides for sperm, the more regularly she ripens eggs that can be fertilized—all of this could be compared to the number of prizes being offered in a lottery. And the quality and number of sperm that the husband possesses correspond to the number of tickets purchased in the lottery. The more of these circumstances that a couple has in their favor, the better their chances of conceiving.

It should also be remembered that the more prizes being offered, the fewer tickets one would need to have to stand a chance of winning a prize. And the more tickets one holds, the more chance there is of winning despite fewer prizes being offered. So, too, with couples trying to have a baby: One partner's low degree of fertility may be compensated to some extent by the other partner's high fertility.

When the fertility of *both* the husband and the wife is fairly low, it may be that in the number of years allotted them they simply haven't enough chances between them to conceive. But we are dealing here with the *chance* of conceiving. In a lottery, it often happens that a person who buys just one ticket wins the grand prize, while another person can buy a hundred tickets and fail to win anything —though his chances of winning were greater. In the same way, a couple with lower fertility may be lucky enough to conceive often, while a couple with higher fertility may be less lucky.

There have been many couples who suddenly, after years of inability to conceive—for no reason that can be explained—proceed to conceive and bear children one after another.

INVESTIGATING CAUSES OF INFERTILITY

The fertility examination. When a couple with a fertility problem goes to a doctor for help, what should they expect?

First, the doctor will want to know something about past medical history. Did either the husband or the wife have any disease or infection which might have lowered fertility? Is there any history of glandular disturbance? What are the couple's sex habits, frequency of intercourse, sex-hygiene practices?

Next will come a careful physical examination of both husband and wife for any physical defects that may be causing infertility. The doctor will examine the husband's genital organs and semen for any deficiency or abnormality. He will perform a detailed pelvic examination to determine if the wife has normally developed organs, and search for signs of glandular imbalance or deficiency, cysts or tumors.

Unless some other very definite source of infertility is disclosed, the doctor will have the couple return to his office at a favorable time of the month, one or two days after they have had intercourse. He can then check on whether a good number of active sperm from the husband have been able to survive in the wife's cervical mucus.

The doctor will also want to be sure that the wife's Fallopian tubes are open, providing passage for sperm and egg. He will check this by means of the Rubin Test or X rays (see below).

Once the doctor has found that the tubes are open, that the husband's sperm is adequate, that there is no obvious anatomical interference with fertility, and that the wife's cervical mucus is favorable for sperm survival, he will want to know if the wife ovulates—that is, does she produce an egg. The usual method of getting some evidence of this is by the use of the basal temperature curve. This is obtained by having the wife take her temperature each day and keeping a record of how her temperature fluctuates (see page 46). There are other methods, such as taking vaginal smears at regular intervals, or determining the microscopic character of the lining of the uterus, which undergoes certain changes if ovulation has taken place. But the basal temperature curve is still the most common—and easiest—method.

If none of these examinations and tests reveal anything specific that is causing the infertility, the next step would depend on how long the couple have been trying to conceive. If they have only been trying for less than a year and have come for assurance, many doctors will be inclined to let the matter rest there for a time. The couple can continue trying, with the assurance that everything appears normal. But if the couple have been trying for more than a year, the doctor will continue to work on the problem with them, seeking by trial and error to discover what is interfering with this couple's fertility, and what can be done about it. As has been pointed out, it then becomes an individual research problem to be worked out by the doctor and this particular couple.

The Rubin Test and X rays. One method of finding out whether a woman's tubes are open enough to allow her egg to descend is by passing gas through the tubes and observing the pressure. Many women have heard that this is terribly painful. It isn't. There is usually only a mild crampy sensation. If there is resistance to the passage of gas, the tubes may go into a spasm—a sensation quite like a menstrual cramp.

Once this spasm passes, in a normal case, there is practically no sensation at all.

After the test is over and you stand up, the bubbles of gas rise to the highest point they can reach in the abdomen and collect under the diaphragm. This causes an irritation that produces a slight aching pain in the shoulder, usually the right shoulder. Since the diaphragm, where the bubbles collect, is near the lowest ribs, you might expect to feel the ache there. But during the development of the human embryo, the diaphragm originates in one of the gill clefts up in the region of the neck. When it descends to the position which it finally occupies, it brings its nerve supply with it from the higher level. As a result, any irritation of the diaphragm is referred up to the level at which the diaphragm originated—the neck and shoulder region.

The Rubin Test takes from five to ten minutes. It is usually done within a week after the end of a menstrual period. The first reason for this is to make sure that there is no chance of disturbing an egg that has already been fertilized. If the test is made too long a time after the end of the period, the gas may be sent up the tube while a fertilized egg is trying to descend or implant in the uterus—in which case the test would be interfering with conception. Another reason for performing the test at this time is that, shortly after the end of the period, the lining of the uterus is not so thick as later in the month. As a result it is not so likely to cause as much obstruction to the passage of the gas.

There is nothing complicated or mysterious about the Rubin Test. A narrow tube is placed in the cavity of the uterus. Carbon dioxide is allowed to pass into the uterus and upward into the tubes. The doctor simply notes how much pressure is required for the gas to be able to flow through the tubes. From this he can tell whether the tubes are open, closed, or partially blocked (see page 47).

The reason carbon dioxide gas is used is that it is nontoxic, more quickly absorbed, and will not cause bubbles if it gets into a blood vessel.

In some cases it is considered desirable to obtain more information than is revealed by the Rubin Test. A liquid that is opaque to X rays is injected into the uterus in much the same way as gas is introduced in the Rubin Test. As the liquid is injected, a series of X-ray pictures are taken. These show, first, the filling of the cavity of the uterus, revealing any irregularities in its lining.

As the fluid flows into the tubes, it demonstrates not only their shape and position, but whether or not obstruction is present and where it is located.

Temperature charts—their use and abuse. The basal temperature curve is a method of discovering if and when a woman ovulates.

If a normally menstruating, normally ovulating woman takes her temperature on awakening, at about the same time each day, she will find that her temperature tends to be a bit lower than 98 degrees up to the time of ovulation and about one degree higher afterward. The exact temperature isn't important. What is important is that the curve of these temperatures will show a *fairly* straight line until ovulation, then a fairly abrupt rise, and then another *fairly* even line at the higher level. The day before menstruation, the temperature drops again.

This is a very useful method of determining if and when a woman ovulates. It involves no discomfort, no great trouble or expense, and it can be repeated month after month. But it has been badly abused when its usefulness has been misunderstood.

Too frequently it has been used as a guide to intercourse. This is bad psychologically because it makes sex a duty. All spontaneity is lost. A couple worried about fertility already have a strain on the marital tie. If the joy is taken out of sex relations the strain is increased. Husbands have been reduced to virtual impotence by this regulation of lovemaking.

Such use of a temperature chart is pointless, even where there is no bad psychological result. You can never tell when ovulation is taking place, or is going to take place, in any given month by means of a temperature curve. You can only find evidence of when it *has* taken place. By then it is usually too late to fertilize an egg.

It is claimed that there is a drop in temperature at the time of ovulation, just before the abrupt rise in temperature that has been mentioned. But there is no way in which you could make use of that so-called drop, because your temperature does not run on an exactly straight line at any time. It tends to fluctuate within narrow limits, and there is no way to tell which particular drop will be followed by the ovulation rise.

It is true that by keeping a temperature chart for many

months you may learn when you could usually expect ovulation to occur. But no couple who have intercourse with normal frequency will fail to achieve pregnancy just because they keep missing the proper time. Unless they are deliberately following a definite pattern that avoids the fertile period, they are bound to hit the right time sooner or later.

The temperature record should be kept only for the use of the doctor, to help him find out if you ovulate regularly and to guide him in future therapy.

SOME CAUSES OF INFERTILITY

Blocked tubes. If a woman's Fallopian tubes are absolutely sealed, she will remain hopelessly sterile unless she has surgical treatment. Many operations have been devised to correct obstruction in the tubes, but the rate of success has been low. A couple should agree to such an operation only with full realization that it may not succeed in solving the problem, prepared for disappointment if it comes. But if a couple want to have a child, such an operation is certainly worth trying. It gives them a chance to have a baby where they had no chance before.

If there is only some delicate filmy adhesion causing obstruction of the tubes, it is possible that the pressure exerted by the gas of the Rubin Test itself may force the tubes open. And they may remain open long enough for pregnancy to take place. If, instead of the Rubin Test, X-ray examination of the tubes is made, the injected dye may have the same effect.

Cervical mucus unfavorable to sperm. The cervix secretes a mucus that keeps sperm alive inside a woman and provides a fluid through which the sperm can swim upward to reach the egg and fertilize it. Failure to produce a favorable type of mucus in the middle portion of the menstrual cycle—when the egg is ripe and ready for fertilization—can be the cause of infertility. The sperm either die in the vagina, or if they survive at all in the scanty, tenacious mucus that is provided, they remain practically motionless.

There are things that can be done to help this condition. Cervical mucus is under the influence of the ovarian hormones. Estrogen can be used to make the mucus more favorable to sperm survival. The difficulty, for the doctor, is in finding the proper dose of estrogen for each individual woman. It must be enough to stimulate more abundant and favorable cervical mucus secretion, but not so much that it will inhibit the pituitary gland and thus prevent formation of an egg. If it is chronic infection of the cervix that is rendering the mucus unfavorable, local cauterization—with or without antibiotics or sulfa drugs—may cure the condition.

Glandular disturbances. Disturbances of the thyroid, the pituitary gland, the ovaries, or the adrenal gland can interfere with menstrual cycles or ovulation—and thus impair fertility. Some of these glandular disturbances can now be corrected with hormone treatments or stimulating doses of X rays. In rare cases, disturbance may be due to glandular tumors, requiring surgical removal.

Abortions. Infection following an abortion can cause blocking of the tubes. For this reason, if for no other, a woman should never take the idea of an induced abortion lightly. It may cause an infection, blocked tubes, and ruin her chance of ever having a baby.

Past illnesses. Illnesess and infections—among them tuberculosis of the uterus or tubes, peritonitis, mumps—may cause infertility or absolute sterility. But many of these infections, which in the old days caused sterility, are now cured by antibiotics at such an early stage that no such harmful effect on fertility occurs.

Age. After a woman reaches thirty or thirty-five, her chances of conceiving begin *gradually* to lessen. There are many women who do conceive quite easily in their forties. But in most cases, fertility does decline with aging until a woman reaches menopause and can no longer conceive at all. With men, the evidence is less clear. A man seems to remain fertile as long as he is potent.

MISCONCEPTIONS ABOUT CONCEPTION

"Infantile" womb. Many a pregnant woman has said in great surprise, "I never expected to conceive so quickly because I was told I had an infantile uterus." There is no question that the term "infantile uterus" or "infantile womb" has been used too freely. Many women have been led to believe that their uterus is infantile when it is not.

There *is* such a thing as an infantile uterus. If a woman's uterus is truly infantile, the chances of conception are very slim indeed. It is not just a matter of the size of the uterus. It mean that there is something wrong with her whole genital development. Hormone treatments are of little value. Increasing the size of the uterus with hormones cannot improve the functioning of the ovaries and the pituitary gland. If anything, it would further depress the functioning of the pituitary—which is the gland that stimulates the ovaries to produce hormones in the first place.

But relatively few women do have an infantile uterus. Many women have a *small* uterus, but unless it is markedly underdeveloped there is no reason why this should interfere with fertility. There is a wide variation in the size of the uterus just as there is a wide variation in the height of people who can still be considered normal. A woman may have a uterus that is smaller than what is considered average, and be perfectly capable of conceiving and bearing children.

Tipped womb. When a woman stands, her womb (uterus) normally lies forward, almost horizontal, with the top of her womb near the bladder. But in about 20 per cent of women the uterus lies with the top part back toward the rectum, and this is perfectly normal for them. This is "retroversion," the well-known tipped womb.

There is a popular impression that this is an important cause of infertility. But there is little evidence that this is so —unless it is an abnormal retroversion due to previous infection that resulted in adhesions binding the uterus in that position.

Hyperacidic vagina. The hyperacidic vagina is an old wives' tale. One popular theory was that in some women the vagina produced acids that were unfavorable to sperm. To cope with such a problem, it was suggested that a woman use a douche that would counteract the acids in her vagina—or that artificial insemination with the husband's semen be used to by-pass the hostility of the vaginal acids.

But the vagina is *normally* hostile to sperm. This is the prod to get the sperm to leave the vagina as promptly as possible, escaping upward into the cervical mucus. It is the cervix that was intended to offer a favorable medium for sperm survival, not the vagina.

Pre-control of a baby's sex. There have been and still are many methods being propounded for controlling the sex of a child-to-be. It has been claimed that you can have a boy or a girl, whichever you wish, by having intercourse at the right time of the month or by using certain douches before intercourse. Not one of these theories has been substantiated.

MALE INFERTILITY

A virile man is not necessarily a fertile man. When this was truly a man's world, it was believed that if a couple did not have a baby it was always the wife's "fault." This belief persists among the uninformed today. It is not true. When a couple are unable to have children, the infertility lies with the husband as often as with the wife. And there is absolutely no connection between a man's virility and his fertility. A man may be very virile in appearance, quite potent, have no past history of infection or illness, be completely normal in every other respect—and still be infertile or absolutely sterile.

Mechanical causes. Sometimes the cause of a man's infertility is mechanical. There can be an obstruction in one of the ducts that carry sperm from the testicles to the passage in the penis. These ducts may have been closed by inflammation. The sperm are formed, but they cannot escape from the testicles.

When a doctor finds that there are no sperm at all in a husband's ejaculation, investigation is undertaken to find out if there is such an obstruction. If this proves to be the trouble, the husband may be helped by surgery, which opens the ducts.

But this cause of infertility is comparatively rare. More usually the fault lies in a deficiency of the sperm production.

Insufficient numbers of sperm. A man's semen may be deficient in a number of ways. The quantity or quality of sperm may be too low.

There is a wide range within which numbers of sperm seem to make little difference. A man with one hundred million sperm may be as fertile as a man with five hundred million. But if the sperm count becomes *too* low, fertility is reduced.

The sperm count may be too low for many reasons, including poor general health, a bout of mumps that affected the testicles, exposure to radiation or industrial poisons. The popular idea that it can be caused by drinking does not seem to be true. There is no evidence that alcohol itself, except when it is a reflection of poor living habits, would reduce sperm count.

Normal men may have their sperm counts reduced to zero temporarily, even by such apparently trifling illnesses as chicken pox, and the count will rise to normal again. But if the level of sperm is persistently too low it is a different matter. No way has been found so far to increase the number of sperm by any specific treatment. The advice of a doctor will be to observe good living habits, get sufficient exercise, have a proper diet, correct overweight or underweight—in other words, to do everything possible to improve general physical condition. After that, time may or may not allow the husband with a low sperm count to have children. His chances are poorer than those of a man with normal numbers of sperm, but there is still a chance.

Poor-quality sperm. There are men in whom the sperm, though adequate in numbers, are sluggish in activity, a great many of them perhaps motionless. The doctor will study the husband's sperm to see what percentage of them possesses any motion at all, and what percentage appears to be dead. He will also examine the amount of activity in those sperm that do move. Do they just move listlessly, staying pretty much in the same place, or are they able to propel themselves from place to place?

If a man's sperm are relatively inactive—that is, if some of his sperm do possess motion—the doctor may be able to help. Improving the man's general health is always the first step. And there has been recent work indicating that the quality of sperm activity can be improved by the use of the male sex hormone. Treatment with male hormone generally tends to reduce the numbers of sperm. But the number does not seem to be so important as activity.

Frequency of intercourse and sperm quality. It has often been suggested that couples who are having trouble conceiving should have intercourse only during the fertile period, on the theory that the husband could thus stock-pile good sperm.

This notion is contradicted by the more recent findings. Although repeated intercourse seems to lower the numbers of sperm (but not below the fertile level), it does not lower the quality or activity of the sperm that are present. And, as was mentioned in the previous section, the latest research indicates that it is the activity and quality of sperm, rather than their numbers, which govern chances of conception.

Artificial insemination with the husband's semen. Introducing the husband's semen into the wife's vagina artificially is done at times when the husband is impotent, incapable of penetration, or ejaculates prematurely. It has also been done in cases where the husband had a poor-quality semen, in the hope that there would be a better chance of conception than with the natural method, where most of the semen escapes almost immediately.

Adoption versus artificial insemination with unknown donor. When the husband is completely sterile the only recourse for a couple who want a child is adoption or—if there is no reason to doubt the wife's fertility—artificial insemination of the wife with the semen of a donor whose identity is kept secret. Many doctors perform such insemination. Whether it is moral or ethical is up to the individual to decide. Its legality has never been officially determined. Some judges have held that a child of such artificial insemination is illegitimate and must be adopted by the husband to become his legitimate heir.

A doctor cannot guarantee, of course, that artificial insemination will result in pregnancy any more than anyone can guarantee that natural intercourse will. And he cannot guarantee a normal offspring any more than he could when conception has occurred naturally.

There are many reasons why couples seek artificial insemination. Adoption is difficult. The wife may want the experience of "having a baby." Some couples will be able to have more pride in having a baby of "their own"—since no one but the doctor need know that they resorted to artificial insemination with a donor.

The doctor has to be certain that a couple are able to cope with the tricky emotional complications of artificial insemination with a donor. Many a husband will feel that a child by such artificial insemination will be less his own than his wife's—that they would at least share equally in an adopted child. Sometimes the wife, too, will feel that the child is hers and not her husband's. Despite this, some men feel that if they cannot father a child, at least they want one who may have their wife's characteristics.

In many cases, when the couple have been anxious for artificial insemination with a donor, and when the doctor has taken sufficient time to make sure that the couple are psychologically able to handle the situation, it has worked out well.

Whether a couple adopt or use artificial insemination, they should remember: It is raising a child that makes him yours, not giving him birth.

INFLUENCE OF EMOTIONS ON FERTILITY

The emotional content of marriage. Because the emotional content of a marriage bears so heavily on the question of fertility and sterility, a doctor dealing with a couple who are having a fertility problem cannot just treat one part of the husband or wife and let it go at that. Fertility work is not veterinary medicine. You have to treat the whole person.

The doctor will try to evaluate the marital relationship, sex adjustment, causes of tensions. He will tread delicately in making suggestions about the couple's sex life, because a marriage with a fertility problem is a strained marriage. The last thing the doctor wants to do is to increase this strain. If a couple become tense about their sexual activities, it will hamper what the doctor is trying to do.

Sex practices that may interfere with conception. The doctor will want to know something about the sex drive of an infertile couple. There are couples who have intercourse only once or twice a month. It would be easy for them consistently to miss conception. If a couple have intercourse so seldom, the time when they are most likely to have the desire is right after menstruation, when they have not had intercourse for a while. Then, if easily satiated, they would be most likely to have intercourse again just before the next period. Thus they would miss the wife's fertile period, her time of ovulation, each month.

The doctor will want to know about sex customs that might interfere with conception in a particular couple. Orthodox Jews, for example, cannot have intercourse for a week after the end of the wife's menstrual period. If the wife had a long menstrual flow and a short menstrual cycle, they would consistently miss the fertile period.

Habits of sex hygiene are another factor. As an example, there are women who are so fastidious that they will insist on douching after intercourse, even when they want to become pregnant. This certainly would not enhance chances of conception.

Nervous tension. There is no doubt that the emotions can affect chances of conception. First of all, mental tension can lower the sex drive—and the less intercourse a couple has the less chance they have of conceiving. Nervous tension and mental weariness are quite different from physical tiredness in this respect. People can spend a whole day swimming or playing tennis, and come home sleepy and tired—but with plenty of energy left for sexual relations. But if you are worried, distracted, and concerned, if your mind is on your job or something else, it is much more difficult to become aroused sexually. Your emotions cannot be focused properly.

The interweaving of the emotions, sex activity, and the workings of your reproductive organs go even deeper than this. After marriage, for example, many women report that their menstrual cycles and periods have changed. With some women, previously painful periods become less painful after marriage, and irregular cycles become more regular. With others, the opposite happens. Not only sexual activity, but emotional upheavals of any sort may affect menstruation, actually stopping the menstrual period for long intervals of time in some instances.

Since emotional stress can reduce a man's potency, as well as interfere with a woman's menstrual cycle and ovulation, the emotional content of a marriage certainly can influence chances of having a baby. This is not only true of humans. We know that many wild animals cannot be bred in captivity, even when maintained in perfect physical health.

Of course, neurotic couples do become successfully and repeatedly pregnant. But it is also true that some individuals under nervous tension develop ulcers, while other individuals never develop an ulcer no matter what the stress. They react, they're just as upset, but their response is not that of producing an ulcer. So, too, you might say that some individuals will react to nervous tension with some mechanism that interferes with fertility, while others under the same stress do not.

Where nervous tension does lower fertility, the reasons are too deep to be cured simply by saying relax, go out and enjoy yourself, and get pregnant. That will not help fertility any more than you can heal a person's ulcer by telling him to stop worrying.

Couples with a fertility problem are frequently advised to take a vacation on the assumption that this will relax them enough so they will be able to conceive. Sometimes it happens that way. A vacation is a fine thing for anybody. But the idea of specifically recommending a vacation is bad. A vacation with a specific purpose, a vacation during which something of vital importance must be accomplished, is no longer a vacation.

Influence of the orgasm on conception. Certainly, if a man has no orgasm, conception cannot take place, since the discharge of semen occurs with his orgasm. But as far as the woman is concerned, there is no evidence to show that the female orgasm is necessary for conception. There is proof that conception can occur without female orgasm—as with women who have conceived by artificial insemination.

Does adoption help couples conceive? Almost everyone knows of a couple who adopted a child and subsequently had one of their own. Apparently, the belief that adopting a child will increase your chances of conceiving goes back to antiquity. The idea at one time was that adoption was a good deed, and that therefore you were rewarded with a child of your own.

Today it is less of a good deed than a good break to be able to adopt a child. Now the feeling is that, since having an adopted child enables a couple to be less tense in their desire for pregnancy, the couple's chances of conceiving are improved.

It is hard to collect valid statistics on this. There are some studies that show the opposite. Fewer children were born to couples who had adopted children. But these statistics are misleading. Adoption agencies naturally tend to favor the couples who are most hopelessly sterile.

All that can be said is that there is no scientific proof that adoption improves a couple's chance of pregnancy. I know of one case where the opposite occurred. This couple had tried to have a baby for years, without success. They arranged to adopt a baby, and were notified that the baby would arrive the following week. They got everything ready for the new arrival in a frenzy of happiness, furnished a lovely nursery in their home. Then, the day before the baby was to arrive, they received a telegram that the adoption had been canceled. The baby would not arrive. It was the very month after this happened that the couple conceived at last, and they subsequently had a child of their own for the waiting nursery.

CHAPTER 4

When You Become Pregnant

SIGNS OF PREGNANCY

The first clues. As soon as a menstrual period is significantly delayed, the woman who has been trying to conceive begins to look for symptoms that will confirm her hopes. At this early stage there may be no symptoms at all, except that the usual pre-menstrual sensations appear unusually strong.

If you have been able, in the past, to tell that a period was due because of certain pre-period symptoms, you will usually have exactly the same symptoms when you become pregnant—except that your period does not appear. Or, if a period does come, it is only a very slight staining, rather than the usual flow. Instead of the symptoms disappearing in a day or two as menstrual flow increases, if you are pregnant the staining will disappear and the symptoms will increase.

The breasts become more and more sensitive, especially in the outer portions, near the arms. There is a tingling sensation around the nipples. Occasionally a drop of secretion may be expressed from the breasts even as early as a week after a period has been missed.

Within another week or so, as the period is further delayed, there may be a noticeable increase in the frequency of urination.

Some women will begin to have feelings of dizziness or nausea. This is popularly called "morning sickness," since it customarily appears early in the morning. But it may appear at any time, or persist throughout the day. It may happen in the evening when you are more tired, since it is often aggravated by fatigue.

But many women have no symptoms in early pregnancy;

no nausea, no increased desire to urinate, no special breast signs. For them the only clue that they have conceived is the continued absence of menstruation.

A woman's own sensations can sometimes lead her to believe that she has become pregnant when she has not, and that she is not pregnant when she actually is.

When there is some ovarian disturbance—possibly there has been no production of an egg that month—and the period is delayed, a woman is quite often certain she has become pregnant. She'll tell her doctor, "I didn't get my period and I don't have a feeling I'm going to get my period." In these cases, she is usually not pregnant.

On the other hand, when a woman has conceived, from the moment her menstrual period is due she will often begin to have all the symptoms which she normally associates with the beginning of a period. She'll tell her doctor, "I feel as if I'm going to get my period any minute, so I'm sure I'm not pregnant." She may go on saying this for two or three weeks, until other signs appear that finally convince her that she really is pregnant.

Period-time staining after conception. Sometimes, even though a woman has conceived, she will have what seems to be the beginning of a menstrual flow at the time when the period is due. In about 25 per cent of all pregnancies there is some amount of bleeding during the first two or three months of pregnancy.

In some animals this is routine. It is called the "placental sign." It is caused by the burrowing of the placenta (afterbirth) into the lining of the uterus, which causes some leakage of blood.

In the human being, this is never regarded as normal, although it does occur often, especially at the time the first menstrual flow is expected after conception. It is usually just a slight staining. Nevertheless, it must always be viewed as a possible threat. But such staining does happen in one out of every four pregnancies. And two thirds of these women will carry through without any difficulty at all. Only about one out of three of these cases is apt to terminate in miscarriage.

False pregnancy. Any woman may of course begin to imagine some of the symptoms of pregnancy if a period has been delayed and there is anxiety about it. This, however is not what is meant by false pregnancy, or *pseudo-*

cyesis, a special condition affecting menopausal women. They generally put on weight and insist they feel life. It calls for psychiatric treatment.

PROOF OF PREGNANCY

Internal examination. A doctor who has examined you before pregnancy may be able to tell fairly definitely whether you are pregnant as early as two weeks after you have missed a period. Knowing what your organs are like normally, he can often detect even very small changes that have taken place. In some cases he might be able to tell even sooner than two weeks after the missed period. If the doctor you go to has not examined you before, it would usually be three weeks or longer before he could be positive of pregnancy on the basis of an internal examination alone.

Women often wait until they are about to skip a second period before going to a doctor. One reason is that they themselves are not sure they are pregnant, and they don't know whether a doctor can be absolutely sure. If they have no unusual symptoms, if they are comfortable, there is certainly no reason for them to go any earlier.

However, women should not be prejudiced against going because of fear that an internal examination will cause a miscarriage. This fear is common—and unfortunate. Because of it, many women will not go to see a doctor if they think they are pregnant and are staining slightly. If they do go to a doctor, they don't want him to examine them. Such fear is completely without basis. If there are unusual symptoms, an early examination is most important. Something of a serious nature may be missed by delaying.

If you have missed your period by only a week or so, think you are pregnant, and otherwise have no unusual symptoms, you would not need a pelvic examination. You might as well wait two or three weeks, by which time a positive diagnosis of pregnancy can often be made by internal examination alone. But you *must* not delay if you have any unusual symptoms.

Pregnancy tests. Since a doctor can usually determine whether you are pregnant by examining you a few weeks after you have missed a period, there is little reason for most women to resort to one of the pregnancy tests. These are used when a woman is extremely anxiously anxious to know whether she is pregnant. They are also used in cases where an abnormality, such as a tubal pregnancy, is suspected; in such a case the sooner the doctor finds out what is going on, the better. There are conditions under which the doctor could not be absolutely certain that a woman is pregnant by examination alone until she has missed her period by four to six weeks.

Most pregnancy tests are biological in nature. They depend on the fact that the urine of a woman who is pregnant contains increased pituitary-like hormone. This hormone is excreted into the urine in increased amounts as early as the time of the missed period, or even slightly before. It reaches its highest concentration at about three months of pregnancy. After that it diminishes somewhat.

There are many animals that will show a response to urine that contains this increased amount of hormone. The original A-Z Test is performed with immature mice. An injection of urine from a pregnant woman causes changes in the ovaries of the mice. Immature rats can be used in the same way.

The popular Friedman modification—the well-known "rabbit test"—depends on the fact that an unmated female rabbit will ovulate if urine from a pregnant woman is injected into its ear vein. The ovary of the rabbit is examined. If the woman is pregnant, a blood spot will be found in the ovary. The test usually takes twenty-four hours; if the doctor wants to be more certain, he may wait forty-eight hours before examining the rabbit's ovary.

Recently, attempts to find cheaper animals have led to the use of frogs. But these have proved less reliable.

No biological test is accurate 100 per cent of the time. The rabbit test is about 90 to 95 per cent accurate. The frog test doesn't do better than about 80 to 85 per cent. There are relatively few false *positive* results, indicating that a woman is pregnant when she is not—except when there is a laboratory error, or when a woman is going through menopause. False negative reports, however, can occur at any stage of pregnancy, with any test. A certain animal may simply not respond to a particular dose of hormone. Or a specific dose of urine may contain too weak an amount of hormone to result in a positive pregnancy report.

There are also chemical tests of various types, but they are less reliable than the biological tests.

One test that has again received publicity is the colostrum test, which is neither chemical nor biological in the usual sense. More than twenty years ago it was first claimed that if this precursor of human breast milk is injected into the skin of a woman who is *not* pregnant it will produce an area of inflammation. A woman who *is* pregnant does not react to the injected colostrum.

This test proved unreliable in the past. Whether newer techniques have improved it still remains to be seen.

PART II

Pregnancy

CHAPTER 5

You and Your Obstetrician

HOW TO CHOOSE AN OBSTETRICIAN

What kind of obstetrician? When you become pregnant you face the problem of finding an obstetrician—unless you have already been under the care of one, or your family doctor is handling your pregnancy and delivery.

All of your women friends who are already mothers will be eager to solve this problem for you—each insisting that the obstetrician who delivered her baby is the best there is. The devoted loyalty of a woman to her obstetrician is almost fanatic in intensity.

There are two extremes in attitude toward relief from pain during delivery: "painless" childbirth and "natural" childbirth. The methods of most obstetricians are somewhere between these two opposite extremes.

If one of your friends has had a baby by "painless" childbirth, she may say that any doctor who lets you feel a labor pain is a barbarian out of the Middle Ages. She'll tell you that her doctor had her in the hospital before labor started, put her to sleep before she had a single labor pain, and when she woke up she had a baby.

The proponents of "natural" childbirth, on the other hand, may tell you that a doctor who uses *any* drugs in delivery is a charlatan. Use of drugs, they say, may cause the birth of a baby with a severely damaged brain, if living at all. Even if the child is normal, you will have less affection for it because you were not "there" when it was born. And, since childbirth is not naturally painful, why miss the greatest experience of your life?

It can be pretty confusing. Where is the truth?

"Painless" childbirth. The pain-relieving drugs available today—if used with judgment—can do more than make birth more comfortable for the mother. They can actually make delivery safer for both mother and child.

For pain, like other protective reactions of the body, can become so extreme that it becomes a threat itself. The woman who has suffered long hours of unrelieved pain approaches a state of exhaustion and is more susceptible to shock. And if exhaustion makes it impossible for her to co-operate, it can make for a much more difficult delivery. This means more danger to the child.

But pain-relieving medication must be used properly. This means more than that the obstetrician must be aware of the safe limits of the drug he uses. It also means that he must give constant, careful attention to the progress which a woman is making in labor and ration out the drug accordingly. It is not wise to give a woman drugs at too early a stage of labor, when her contractions are mild and when she could easily be encouraged to carry on without drugs. For if medication is given too early, more and more of it will be called for as the pains grow more severe. Finally, just at the time when the contractions are strongest and the effect of pain-relieving medication is most needed, the safe amount of drug that can be given to the woman has already been used up. Since spinal or caudal anesthesia is not always available or desirable, the obstetrician may be faced with two unfortunate choices: To let the woman suffer these severe pains without relief; or to exceed the dose which he knows to be safe and risk depressing the respiratory centers of the infant's brain.

It is for this reason that women may have to feel the cramps of early labor—which may go on for many hours before progressive labor begins. Usually, such cramps are only mildly uncomfortable. But if the woman is tired out by their persistence, the doctor will give her enough medication to afford a few hours' sleep.

On the other hand, labor should not be allowed to go on

until the limit of tolerance for pain has been reached, if medication is to achieve its best effect. The medication is given as soon as labor is sufficiently advanced. For if one waits too long, by the time drugs are used labor may have progressed too rapidly for the medication to take effect before delivery. If this happened, the woman would receive little relief, except from anesthesia at the time the child is born.

When drugs are properly used, there is no question that labor can be made at least comfortable enough so that every woman with normal pain tolerance will face future labors calmly. But the conscientious obstetrician will admit that he cannot guarantee that every single one of his patients will recall no pain at all. Probably 80 to 85 per cent will recall no pain of any great severity in the course of labor or birth. But these are women with normal susceptibility to drugs. The amount of drug that would be required to produce oblivion in some women may be three or more times the dose that brings relief to the normally susceptible.

In order to bring complete relief to all his patients, the obstetrician would have to give some patients a greater amount of medication than he considers safe. Even where this increased dose may be safe for the mother, it may prove dangerous for the child being born. There is no reason to believe that just because the mother has a great tolerance for a certain medication, her infant will also possess this greater tolerance.

Women should be given as much relief from pain as is compatible with the safety of mother and child. Our first concern is the safety of the mother, our second the safety of the child; only in third place comes comfort and painlessness.

All the above is quite different—in degree at least—from the methods employed by that small group of obstetricians who have won themselves a special reputation for painlessness. These men promise each and every patient complete oblivion.

Even they, of course, could not live up to this promise 100 per cent of the time, because with some women a lethal dose of drug might be required. However, they certainly have succeeded in producing complete oblivion for a very high percentage of the women who come to them by using drugs more liberally than conservative obstetricians consider wise, and recently by adding to this the routine induction of labor—that is, by bringing on the labor artificially before nature starts any labor pains.

It should be obvious that no obstetrician today has any secret method of relieving pain, or a monopoly on any particular drug. The obstetrician who promises complete oblivion to all his patients has only one thing that other obstetricians do not have: He has more courage when it comes to risking possible ill effects upon you and your child.

Delivering babies is essentially safe. It remains essentially safe in spite of grave abuses—in most cases. In any large private obstetrical practice there are difficult cases that have an unfortunate outcome. It would be impossible for patients to judge whether use or abuse of any method contributed to that outcome in any particular case.

No obstetrician could survive very long in practice if his mortality rates were very much higher than those of more conservative doctors. But it is significant that none of the men who practice these "painless" methods occupy important teaching positions in medical schools, or as heads of obstetrical departments in large hospitals. For when such methods are applied more widely, to large clinic groups, statistics soon reveal their inherent danger.

Infants show amazing resistance to asphyxia. They can survive without oxygen for a length of time that would be fatal to an adult. When overuse of drugs has had a depressing effect on the centers that control an infant's breathing, the child *may* be revived without harm. But even an infant's nervous tissue is susceptible to damage from lack of oxygen. This is one of the causes of cerebral palsy.

We will have no way of assessing for many years to come how many individuals have suffered damage to their nervous systems, simply because their mothers did not want to know or feel "anything" while giving birth.

"Natural" childbirth. The tradition that pain must accompany birth is a very ancient one. When, in 1847, Dr. Simpson of Edinburgh first used chloroform to ease its final stages, some objected that he was opposing God's will. Yet no less a person than the Queen of England, then already a mother, hastened to avail herself of his services at her next confinement.

Grateful for the brief moments of relief afforded, Victoria made him a knight. Since that time, women everywhere have been looking hopefully to medical science for the discovery of the perfect drug that will eliminate all pain with complete safety for mother and child.

Now, after a hundred years of research, the hope remains largely unfulfilled, and another voice from the British Isles calls upon us to go back and try a new approach to the problem. Dr. Grantly Dick Read, in *Childbirth Without Fear*, argues that with proper education there should be very little need for anesthetic drugs. Pain, he says, is always an indication that something is wrong. Since, in giving birth, a woman is obviously doing what is right for her, she should feel no pain. If she does, it is our civilization that is wrong —having warped her mind with fear of the natural and deformed her body with poor nutrition and inadequate exercise.

The followers of Dr. Read are not numerous percentagewise, but their enthusiasm has spread the word widely. Few patients come to an obstetrician without having heard some mention of "natural" childbirth, and many seek further information. Some are definitely interested, but more merely wish assurance that this is not the method their doctor has in mind for them.

The conscientious obstetrician is reluctant to disparage the Read method no matter how much he may disagree with its basic philosophy. For the influence of Dr. Read has, on the whole, been a healthy one. It is a welcome antidote to the publicity given those "Painless Parkers" of obstetrics who, in order to justify their more radical practices, must, at least by implication, exaggerate the horrors which their patients are spared.

The kernel of truth in Dr. Read's teaching is that there is no substitute for a feeling of deep confidence to make childbirth a satisfying experience, that there are no short cuts to the attainment of this confidence.

Confidence requires the opportunity to confide—the unhurried atmosphere, the attitude of genuine interest on the part of the obstetrician that encourages his patient to discuss all her problems, no matter how remotely connected with his specialty. She needs the feeling that he knows her as a person, not just as a "case," for pregnancy involves the whole person, mentally as well as physically. And, finally, she must grow to regard him as a friend to whom she may turn for reassurance at any time, though the hour be very, very late and the occasion prove embarrassingly trivial.

When such a relationship has been established, a woman enters labor secure in the knowledge that her doctor is anxious to spare her as much suffering as possible; that if she feels pain, there must be a reason why it cannot be safely relieved. Therefore, she can accept it without accusing him of impatience or indifference or neglect.

The recollection of kind and sympathetic care will persist as a warming memory long after the pain of childbirth is forgotten. No amount of medication will serve in its place. The woman who goes into labor feeling alone and afraid may be drugged into insensibility throughout, yet awaken with the sensation of having experienced some vague but terrible nightmare that she hopes will never return.

The Read method endeavors to instill confidence by systematic instruction in the physiological processes of pregnancy and birth. Thus the woman is given a clearer understanding of the changes going on in her body and the various sensations they may be expected to produce. This understanding must be imparted to the husband as well, for without his co-operation the effect may be lost. Anxiety is contagious. (The advocates of "natural" childbirth also urge the husband to stay by his wife's side as long as the hospital will permit, doing whatever he can to make her more comfortable during labor—and even watching the baby delivered in the few hospitals that allow this.)

It is important that the instruction be given in groups, for seeing others undergoing the same experience and hearing them describe the same symptoms are in themselves reassuring. Classes to which the obstetrician may refer his patients are conducted by public-spirited organizations such as the Maternity Center Association in New York City.

In addition to the educational program, patients are given a series of exercises to perform. Some are designed to make carrying the unborn child more comfortable, others to strengthen those muscles that will be called upon in giving birth. Still others, particularly the breathing exercises, have been devised to help the woman achieve relaxation, to help her to avoid tensing her muscles during the first stage of labor when her role is purely passive, allowing the involuntary contractions of the uterus to do all the work. (See Figure H on page 231.)

It is difficult to evaluate the results of this program. Unquestionably, many of its graduates show increased ability to tolerate labor pain and may even deny any suffering at all. But this does not prove that the Read ideal of "childbirth without fear" has been realized. Devoted advocates of natural childbirth frequently believe they are eliminating fear when they are merely substituting. In place of the fear of pain, the pregnant woman may develop a fear of drugs and instruments, a fear that failure to carry through her delivery without drugs will brand her as unworthy of motherhood. Obviously, such an exchange of fears is not necessarily harmless.

Teachers of the Read method are aware of this danger. They try to prevent it by admitting that even their most diligent pupils may feel pain, and that if they require medication, it should not be withheld. But the difficulty is fundamental. One cannot expound the Read dogma that since normal labor is natural it was not "meant to be painful" without evoking a naïve concept of pain as punishment reluctantly administered by an essentially kindly Mother Nature. The association of punishment and humiliation is almost inescapable.

Pain is not a punishment, but a protection. It is one of our most important mechanisms of survival. Pain causes you to withdraw your hand from a hot surface—saving you from a bad burn. The pain of a fracture serves as a natural splint, causing you to hold your injured limb still. By discouraging movement of the broken bones, it prevents further injury.

Although in no way comparable to the pain of a fracture, the pain of the first stage of labor is also an immobilizing pain. The woman who has been walking will suddenly come to a stop, bend over, and grip something when this pain seizes her. As the pains grow stronger and closer together, she will cease moving about. She will want to sit or lie down.

Under modern conditions, such suffering may seem unnecessary. To understand its function we must project ourselves back before the dawn of civilization—before calendars, before tribal organization facilitated accumulation of experience. Then the primitive woman would have had only her inner sensations to force her to give up other urgent pursuits, to seek shelter where her baby might arrive in safety. The sensation would have to be overpowering to make her ignore the pangs of her own hunger and deny the instinct to forage for her crying young. Without the immobilizing birth pangs she might have had her baby while climbing a tree or wading across a river.

Even today rare women who do not experience a sufficient amount of pain in the first stages of labor may endanger their babies. The sudden, violent expulsion of their babies has been known to occur in places such as moving trains, busses, and theaters. The mortality rate would be higher with such women than with those who did have adequate warning that labor was taking place.

That the sensation of labor, though sometimes overwhelming, may be endured in full consciousness needs no proof. More than half the world's population is still unaware that there is any other way. Certainly there is no question that this generation of civilized women is perfectly capable of bearing children without anesthetics or other drugs—just as countless generations of women have done before. However, it may outrage a woman's sense of propriety that in a gleaming hospital, where medical miracles are a daily occurrence, she should be having a baby with the same discomforts that her grandmother knew.

The Read method has helped in dealing with some over-emotional women for whom there is no middle way. Without it, labor may bring a hysterical demand for complete oblivion; with it, an hysterical enthusiasm which nullifies pain. The latter, of course, is infinitely safer.

The Read method may also appeal to the adventurous, who face labor as a personal challenge. Many have found in it an exciting and rewarding experience. But after all the years in which various methods of "natural" childbirth have been practiced, I know of no statistics which indicate that it provides greater safety for mother or child.

The same applies to the "Psychoprophylactic Method" advocated by Fernand Lamaze, a French obstetrician who believes that painless childbirth is entirely possible without drugs, but is highly critical of the Read method, which he considers to be unscientific.

"Psychoprophylaxis" first impressed Dr. Lamaze during a visit to the Soviet Union, where its general application at the time was enforced by a decree of the Ministry of Health. Dr. Lamaze wrote a book on the method, called "Painless Childbirth." It has since been used in some hospitals in America, where it is popularly known as the "Lamaze Method"—

though as used here the method has been changed somewhat, despite Dr. Lamaze's warning against "mongrel methods."

The scientific foundation of the method is to be found in the conditioned reflex research of the famous Russian physiologist Ivan Pavlov. Psychoprophylaxis applies the theory of the conditioned reflex to childbirth.

At the onset of labor, uterine contractions become more regular and increase in intensity until, in the unconditioned woman, they are perceived as pains. But every pregnant woman from the sixth month onward is aware of periodic tightening of the uterus which is not painful. It is at this stage that the psychoprophylactic method begins to train women to associate contractions with special breathing exercises—instead of with pains. She is taught, in a series of lectures, to visualize what is happening with the contractions at each stage of labor, and what voluntary contributions she can make to help the uterus in its work. The breathing exercises learned at the lectures are to be practiced at home in accordance with a definite schedule—30 seconds one day, 35 the next, etc.

By the time the woman goes into labor she has been conditioned so that the strong uterine contraction "signals" rapid, shallow breathing, rather than pain. She enters the hospital promptly, where trained attendants maintain the conditioning with "secondary signals" in the form of verbal instructions. She is taught to relax her muscles between contractions—but not her mind. This must be kept active, for if she becomes drowsy and inattentive, the brain barrier will be lowered and sensations of pain will penetrate.

This method, obviously, demands a high degree of self-discipline. Anyone tempted to try it should first read Marjorie Karmel's entertaining personal account, "Thank you, Dr. Lamaze."

ARE DOCTORS OPPOSED TO NATURAL CHILDBIRTH?

There can be no pleasanter experience for an obstetrician than caring for a woman who is imbued with enthusiasm for natural childbirth and able to carry it off successfully. But he has no way of measuring her spiritual reward or of determining by how much what she chooses to call discomfort differs from what other women call pain.

Without making offensive comparisons it must be obvious that glowing testimonials are not scientific proof. Real progress in medicine must be reflected in cold statistics. At present there are none to indicate that women who elect training for natural childbirth have safer deliveries or healthier babies than a comparable group receiving no such specialized preparation.

Of course medical aspects of natural childbirth are not the only consideration. Bringing a child into the world is more than a clinical experience. Most obstetricians would be happy to encourage any woman who is attracted to the idea of natural childbirth—as long as the attraction is based upon faith, not upon fear. But it would seem to me that such a faith can be only part of a greater faith that every moment of life is worth living, transcending mere physical sensations of comfort or discomfort. Then joy in giving life is the natural reflection of joy in living it.

This is an uncommon quality. One may believe that rare souls such as Dr. Read had the power of imparting it to others, yet still doubt that they knew just how it was done.

Obstetrical fees. How much an obstetrician charges cannot be discussed in terms of absolute amounts. Fees change with the times, vary in different sections of the country, and reflect the doctor's overhead and the financial status of the bulk of his patients. A couple should not allow themselves to be too much influenced by the size of an obstetrician's fees. The doctor who charges a high fee is not necessarily more gifted than one who charges less.

In general, however, the fee represents the amount of time that a doctor gives to the individual patient.

There are obstetricians who customarily charge low fees, preferring a large-volume practice. These obstetricians are naturally not able to give as much personal attention to each of their many patients, or to stay with them any great time during labor. They frequently concentrate their practice in one hospital, so that they can manage to be there at the time of delivery. There is no question that such obstetricians are eminently qualified.

But many women want and require a great deal more personal attention and discussion of their individual problems. They want an obstetrician whose practice is less extensive, so that he has more time for each of his patients. In order to do this, he has to charge a higher average fee.

Each obstetrician, like any other doctor, has an average fee which he charges most patients. Since he is expected to reduce this for those of limited means, the more well-to-do patients may be expected to pay a fee somewhat higher than average. In determining what a particular patient can comfortably afford, an obstetrician cannot evaluate her financial status at a glance, and will not wish to make a searching analysis. He will be influenced in his estimate by her and her husband's occupations, the financial condition of the circle from which the patient has been recommended, and on the type of hospital room that she desires.

You should have no reticence in discussing the fee and method of payment on your first or second visit to your obstetrician. It is the only way to avoid hardship or misunderstanding.

Compatibility. There is no one perfect obstetrician for all women, any more than there is an ideal husband for all. Fortunately, there are different types of both husbands and obstetricians. Each woman has a chance to find one that appeals to her. The priceless ingredient in obstetrical care is the confidence that your obstetrician inspires. There is no substitute for this. The obstetrician is probably unique among specialists in this: It is not just desirable, but absolutely essential that there be a feeling of friendliness between the patient and the doctor.

If your appendix is being removed, although it would be nice if you could regard the surgeon as a friend, the chances are that the surgery will be just as successful whether you like or hate him. But when it comes to guidance through pregnancy and the conduct of labor, this friendliness can actually make the difference between a safe and easy delivery with a co-operative woman and a very difficult and possibly dangerous one with a woman who is not co-operating.

So be sure—*early*—that you like and absolutely trust your obstetrician. If you find you do not, change quickly to another one for your own sake and the sake of the obstetrician.

YOUR FIRST VISIT TO THE OBSTETRICIAN

Getting to know you. For the next ten to twelve months of your life your obstetrician will be the one primarily responsible for your health. While you are pregnant, and for some time afterward, there will be a tendency to interpret your every symptom as possibly having something to do with your pregnancy, and to consult your obstetrician about it.

Naturally, pregnancy does not confer immunity against any disease. Some of the conditions that arise may require treatment by a specialist in some other field. The obstetrician, like any other specialist, is not qualified to treat every condition, nor even to make the final diagnosis of every condition. But because you are pregnant, you will probably turn first to your obstetrician whenever anything seems to be wrong with you. The obstetrician must then know everything about you, your health, and your medical background. He must know what is normal for *you*, in order to be in a position to detect the first signs of any abnormality—to insure prompt and proper treatment, whether by him or another doctor.

First, he will want a complete history of all your past illnesses, operations, and accidents. There are conditions that require special care during pregnancy, or that are likely to flare up; the obstetrician must be alert for such possibilities. The growing uterus, for example, might carry with it an adherent loop of intestine from a previous abdominal operation. This could cause an intestinal obstruction that might not be promptly recognized since nausea and vomiting are so common in pregnancy—unless your doctor has been watching for just such an occurrence.

It is also important for your obstetrician to know your family's medical history. Any history of diabetes, for instance, would be important because this condition might first reveal itself during pregnancy.

The physical examination that follows this history taking is a complete one, from head to toe, including eyes, nose, throat, thyroid gland, heart, lungs, urine examination, blood test, and the hemoglobin determination that will reveal anemia.

Your obstetrician wants you to be in the best possible physical condition throughout your pregnancy. He will try to correct anemia or other defects revealed by this initial examination. Ideally, of course, all health problems should have been corrected before you became pregnant. But much can be done even at this time.

The blood test is extremely important. It is always possible, though not so common today, for a woman to have been infected with syphilis and not know about it. If such a condition is revealed by the blood test, and the woman is treated during pregnancy and cured, her child will be born healthy. If she is not treated, there is always the chance that she may infect the child through the placenta, and the child will be born with what is called congenital syphilis.

The other test performed upon your blood at this time is the blood typing and determination of the Rh factor (see page 104). It is useful to know your blood type as a precaution for any future emergency, when blood transfusions may be required. Although your blood must be retyped and cross-matched at the time of the transfusion, at least you have one previous record of your blood type as a guarantee against possible error should haste be required.

Your obstetrician will note your breast development and type of nipple, especially if you are interested in nursing your baby. If you do decide to nurse, your obstetrician will make a note of it, so that in the last weeks of pregnancy he can show you how to give proper attention to the preparation of your breasts and nipples.

The obstetrician will also observe the character of your veins for any tendency to varicose veins or hemorrhoids. He will not be able to prevent the formation of either, but he will stress those things that aggravate the condition and should be avoided.

Most women, even as early as this first visit, would like the assurance that they have a reasonable chance of a normal delivery—that is, that they are "big enough." The external pelvic measurements usually taken at this time, though not conclusive, can give some idea of the shape and adequacy of your pelvic structure. At this early stage of pregnancy the vagina is not usually sufficiently relaxed to facilitate taking the *internal* measurements that are more informative. These internal measurements are usually deferred to the beginning of the ninth month, since they have no importance until the baby has grown beyond premature size.

Internal examination—other than pelvic measurements—must be done during the first visit. Your obstetrician determines the size and position of your uterus, so that if signs of threatened miscarriage arise later he will be able to evaluate the amount of growth that has taken place and judge whether the pregnancy is thriving. By means of this internal examination the obstetrician can discover not only conditions that may have some serious bearing on the outcome of the pregnancy, but some that may affect your health in general.

Your turn to ask questions. Following this complete examination, your obstetrician will instruct you in the general rules you must follow during pregnancy. These rules will be modified if any special physical defects have been discovered. What medication you receive and what diet you are advised to follow will also depend upon the extent to which you are distressed by nausea.

Then it will be your turn to ask questions about anything that concerns you. During this and subsequent visits do not hesitate to talk to your obstetrician about whatever troubles you. He wants you to have as relaxed a pregnancy as possible. The questions asked of an obstetrician vary from woman to woman. But there are a multitude of questions that seem to concern nearly all pregnant women. These are dealt with in other chapters of this book.

Before you terminate this first visit, you should also discuss the hospital you will go to and the kind of room you desire.

Future visits to your obstetrician will, of course, be of much briefer duration. Your weight and blood pressure will be recorded at each visit, and your urine examined. Other tests or examinations will be performed when indicated, but generally it is only necessary for your doctor to feel your abdomen in order to note whether your pregnancy is developing satisfactorily.

When there are no unusual circumstances, one visit every three or four weeks is considered adequate during the first seven months of pregnancy—with visits at two-weeks intervals in the eighth month and every week in the ninth month.

PLANNING YOUR HOSPITALIZATION

Choosing a hospital. Your choice of hospital will depend upon your choice of obstetrician—just as your choice of an obstetrician may be influenced by a preference for one particular hospital, for few doctors would care to deliver patients in more than two, three, or—at the very most—four hospitals. Each of them may have some advantage or disadvantage as regards accessibility, convenience of visiting hours, or other factors. Your doctor will help you to decide which of the hospitals with which he is connected fits your needs and convenience best.

Distance from the hospital is a source of great concern to many couples. Husbands in particular are apt to conjure up visions of the worst possible travel conditions at the very moment the baby is about to arrive. The thousand of babies born routinely in the hospitals are mentioned in the news only as paid birth announcements, but there are always dramatic feature stories about the few who are born on the way.

It is a rare woman who does not receive hours of warning before birth takes place. Unless you have a history of unusually rapid delivery of a first baby, a hospital that is no more than an hour away is near enough.

Private or semi-private? Hospitals provide two types of accommodation for private patients: one in a room, which is private; or more than one in a room, which is semi-private. Semi-private may consist of two, three, four, or more in a room, since the term "semi-private" merely refers to the fact that you do not have a room to yourself, yet have a private physician taking care of you.

Today there is not a great deal of price differential between semi-private and the least-expensive private rooms. In many hospitals, the total difference in cost for a normal birth would not be more than three or four dollars a day.

Even if you have Blue Cross coverage, the difference in cost for a normal birth would not be greater—since Blue Cross grants only a flat benefit of approximately $80 regardless of the length of your stay. However, if some complication should arise, requiring a Caesarean, the cost differential might be greater—since under these circumstances Blue Cross pays the regular surgical benefits, including allowance for the *full* price of a *semi-private* room.

Nursing care in a semi-private room is normally just as good as in a private room. The food is usually the same.

Your personal feeling about privacy will probably most influence your choice. A private room gives you solitude, and, of course, more privacy in which to enjoy the visits of your family and friends. Also, in a private room you can usually have visitors more frequently.

In a semi-private room you'll have other young women around to keep you company during the greater part of your stay in the hospital. For the more sociable, a semi-private room frequently has a pleasant clublike feeling. The atmosphere is usually a cheerful one. On maternity floors sick patients are the exception rather than the rule as on other hospital floors.

There may also be a difference in regard to labor. In some hospitals there is no essential difference, because all maternity patients are admitted directly to a labor room regardless of the time of day or the activity of the labor. They are not permitted to have their husbands or close relatives with them from the time of admission. But in other hospitals you will be admitted to your own room. If it is a private one, your husband will be allowed to stay with you in your room until labor progresses to the point where it is necessary to transfer you to the labor room. Obviously, this would be impractical in a semi-private room, since patients and their husbands coming in at all hours would disturb the other women.

Delivery at home versus hospital. During the last thirty or forty years there has been a tremendous increase in the number of babies born in hospitals as compared to those born at home.

One hundred years ago, infection was the most feared complication. Hospitals were a prevalent source of infection, since all types of cases were treated in close proximity to women giving birth. In some respects, women were also better off if they were not attended by a doctor, for doctors handled infectious material and did not know about germs and proper sterilization. Even after Pasteur's work revealed the cause of infection and how it could be controlled, wherever patients were gathered together, wherever babies were kept together in one nursery, there was more likelihood that infection would spread from one to the other. Under these circumstances, the woman who was delivered in her own home was less likely to become infected than one delivered in a hospital.

There was considerable agitation until the last ten or fifteen years for the development of completely separate maternity hospitals—where there would be no other types of medical or surgical cases, even on separate floors, to spread infections to new mothers and their babies.

But particularly since the advent of sulpha and the antibiotics, infection is not the fearsome complication it once was. The gravest danger now is hemorrhage. This danger has also been reduced in recent times, although not to the same extent as the danger of infection. Hemorrhage and other complications of pregnancy cannot be properly dealt with in the home. They require the facilities of a modern hospital, the operating room, the blood bank.

If home delivery of babies were once again to become popular, the toll of maternal and infant deaths would rise to approach what it was twenty-five years ago.

Rooming-in. During the last few years a movement has grown up to provide facilities whereby the mother can become better acquainted with her baby during her stay in the hospital. This is known as "rooming-in."

The plan differs in detail in different hospitals that have such facilities. The general principle of the plan is that the baby is in a bassinet at the mother's bedside during most of her stay in the hospital.

Since many new mothers are fearful of handling the baby, are frightened by its strange noises or the movements it may make, a competent nurse must always be in attendance. For this reason, rooming-in units are usually semi-private—about four mothers and four babies to a room, and one nurse in charge of all of them. The nurse will usually take care of the needs of the mothers as well as the babies. She will instruct the mothers in feeding, changing, and general care of their babies. There is usually one central nursery provided for all these babies. The infants are removed to it at night, allowing the mothers uninterrupted sleep except when it is necessary to bring a baby out for breast feeding at 2 A.M.

There is no question that if the nurse in charge is a good teacher, the mothers gain a great deal of confidence in the handling of their babies. For any woman who will not have a trained baby nurse or some other experienced person to help her with the baby after she leaves the hospital, rooming-in could be a very useful period of training. However, in the hospital, as in the home, there are only human beings to choose from in selecting baby nurses to teach new mothers. Some may tend to breed anxiety in the young mother rather than alleviate it.

One of the main arguments in favor of rooming-in is that it permits a family feeling to develop at an earlier stage. But in some cities the Board of Health will not allow the father to handle his new baby, which leaves him out of this early "family feeling." And one of the main disadvantages is that visiting is rigidly restricted with rooming-in, because of the danger of infection being carried into the room. Usually only the father and perhaps one other close relative may visit —gowned and masked for the protection of the babies.

There are young women to whom the idea of rooming-in will appeal. But some of the arguments that attempt to persuade women of its great advantages are to be condemned, for they arouse unnecessary anxiety. Such an argument, for example, is the one that the baby will suffer all sorts of psychological trauma due to lack of affection in a cold and scientific nursery where his own mother is barred.

For the average woman, who will have some help on leaving the hospital, who is not unduly fearful of her ability to take care of an infant, rooming-in serves little purpose. She will certainly be able to get more rest and have more freedom to entertain visitors in the ordinary type of private or semi-private hospital accommodation.

CHAPTER 6

Becoming A Father

There never was any doubt that the pregnant woman needs a husband, but now there is some confusion as to the ways in which he can be most helpful. The husband who with masculine arrogance shrugs off the whole thing as a lot of fuss over nothing—"Chinese women have babies out in the fields"—is unlikely to endear himself. On the other hand, the oversolicitous attitude—"Are you sure it's all right, dear?" —may prove a little wearisome before nine months have gone by.

We have pictured the old-fashioned husband responding to the whispered secret with a whoop of joy and then leaving strictly to the womenfolk the mystery of how this miracle was to be brought about. But modern writing stresses the need for greater participation—a process of male initiation, so that the mystery once considered so far beyond his comprehension can now be shared.

In ancient times even the physicians had little to do with the process of childbirth. It is reported that in the Middle Ages a Dutch physician disguised himself as a woman in order to see a baby born—and was executed for his pains. This harsh sentence may not have been altogether unjust, for a century later, when doctors began to replace midwives, they brought death to thousands on their unclean hands. It wasn't until the mid-nineteenth century that the influence of the Hungarian physician Semmelweiss and his passionate plea for cleanliness began to reduce the scourge of child-bed fever.

The advance of medical science has made childbirth so safe that today many obstetricians will never know a maternal death in a full lifetime of practice. Yet the tradition of danger remains, so that the modern husband is inclined to worry more than his grandfather, who could only trust that with a healthy wife and the grace of God all would be well. Because a husband today is aware of the importance of scientific safeguards in the protection of his wife, he must acquire a certain amount of sound knowledge in order to spare himself needless anxiety which may undermine her confidence.

There are many books on pregnancy which are good sources of knowledge. Magazine articles in general are less reliable. They may tend to feature exaggerated claims representing extreme points of view, since controversy is a great circulation booster. Childbirth preparation classes which husband and wife attend may also be helpful.

At the risk of sentimentalizing, I must state here that scientific knowledge is not everything. That old-fashioned whoop of joy when early suspicions are first confirmed is still more important than anything else. The glow of new beauty which radiates from expectant mothers cannot come entirely from within. It must be in great part a reflection of their husband's happiness.

Of course, it would be highly unrealistic to expect any couple, no matter how much in love, to maintain a state of continuous exultation. Human beings are too complex to experience "pure" emotions. For every great hope fulfilled there is some small desire abandoned. Into the joy of coming motherhood may intrude regret for girlhood left behind. Conflicts such as this can give rise to guilt feelings, with moods of depression and unexplainable floods of tears. At other times, there may be vague irritability due to the changing balance of internal secretions.

It is natural for the poor husband faced with a distressing mood to consider himself the cause, and wonder what he is doing wrong. Attempts to reason her out of it will get him nowhere. If he grows hurt and angry, he will only make things worse. The fortunate husband is the one who is capable of unobtrusively demonstrating his love, and waiting for the mood to pass.

Although pregnancy is a healthy condition, necessary bodily changes are apt to be attended by varying degrees of physical discomfort in perfectly normal women—nausea, certain aches and pains, a tendency to tire easily. Few men are gifted at nursing. Women are born to care for the helpless and seem to have an instinctive understanding of the ill. But man has only an instinctive fear of illness which tries to substitute fussing for sympathy. If his good intentions are met with an unappreciative, "Go away and leave me alone," it is best that he go away—but not too far.

At the times when a wife does not feel up to carrying on her household tasks, the considerate husband will help in any way he can. The sight of a man attempting to do her work makes many women feel uncomfortable. But there are other ways in which a man can spare his wife's energy, boosting her morale instead of letting her feel in some way inadequate—the suggestion that they dine out when she shows no enthusiasm for cooking, the offer to drive instead of letting her take the bus when she has an errand to do, squeezing an allowance for household help into the budget.

The sexual expression of love often acquires a new beauty and renewed ardor in the knowledge of the life it is creating. Yet there will be occasions when because of some minor discomfort or vague apprehension a wife is simply unable to respond to her husband's love-making. If he sulks, he is denying her the assurance of his love at the very moment when she needs it most.

In the later months of pregnancy, the overcautious husband afraid of doing harm may make his wife feel rejected. As she gains weight and begins to "show," she has a greater need to know that she is feminine and desirable. She becomes oversensitive. The sympathetic observation that she looks tired registers as "unattractive." Her jealousy has a low flashpoint. A mere hint of disloyalty is unforgivable.

Not long ago it was the practice in all the better hospitals to separate husband and wife as soon as they entered the maternity floor. The wife disappeared behind the "No Admittance" door of the labor suite, and the husband was herded into a waiting room to sit hour after hour, perhaps even a day and a night—sometimes with no other word than a "We'll let you know."

This routine has always seemed to me unnecessary and barbaric. The husband imagines his wife suffering untold agony behind a door he is forbidden to enter. And the wife, who may be left alone because she is not "active," amid strange surroundings and frightening sounds, gives way to panic before labor has really begun.

The latent phase of labor, when contractions cause relatively little pain, may go on for hours, and at this stage husband and wife may be a great comfort to one another. But in the active phase of labor, when the contractions become stronger, the average woman finds in the presence at her side of the husband she loves only an added strain. She knows that if she allows a pain to contort her features he will suffer—so she is using her strength to support him.

If she is given medication she will now be under the continuous observation of the trained delivery-room staff. If she chooses to use breathing exercises for control of pain, she will find more reassurance in the calm matter-of-factness of the doctor she had learned to trust than in the fervent encouragement of a husband whose knowledge is no greater than her own.

Unfortunately, the husband is once again relegated to his old role of pacing the floor. But now the waiting period is limited, and he can be given some reasonable estimate of when it will end.

The alternative, which has its advocates, is to allow the husband in the delivery room, something which most doctors deem unwise even when the husband is himself a physician.

Far better than a husband's helpless presence at this time is the strong knowledge of his protecting love, in which a woman finds security with no loss of personal dignity. To believe in the equality of the sexes is to believe in a womanly pride as worthy of respect as masculine pride. The battle for women's rights has been won. It is freely acknowledged that women are the intellectual equals of men, and given the same training can develop the same skills. Now we can afford to recognize that there are differences—and cherish them.

Whether childbirth has been difficult or easy for the wife, with medication or without medication, matters very little in her moment of unshared glory—when she can say to her husband: "Look at your child, which *I* have brought you."

There is glory enough for the man in the act of faith which has placed these lives in his hands.

CHAPTER 7

The Progress of Pregnancy

DURATION OF PREGNANCY

When can you expect your baby? The time-honored rule of thumb by which you can calculate the arrival of your baby is simple: Add seven days to the beginning of your last period and count back three months.

If your last period began July first, you'd add seven days—July 8. Then count back: June, May, April. Your baby would be due about April 8.

This rule was based on the idea that pregnancy was 280 days and that conception took place soon after a period. Actually, we now know that ovulation takes place later in the normal twenty-eight-day cycle: on about the fourteenth day after the onset of a period. But even if you knew the exact date on which conception occurred, you couldn't calculate the probable date of labor any more closely than you can with this old rule. Pregnancy does not last any exact number of days.

Obviously, pregnancy may terminate at any time short of 280 days. If it terminates very early it is known as an abortion, or miscarriage. Later on, once the infant is sufficiently developed to have a chance of survival, it is called a premature birth. Finally, when the baby is more than eight months and more than five pounds, it is considered a normal, full-term birth.

The question about which there is most misunderstanding is whether or not it is actually possible to carry *more* than 280 days. Everyone knows of women who have carried two, three, or four weeks beyond the date originally given as the end of the ninth month. Most people insist that there must have been some error in calculation—possibly due to some menstrual irregularity—and that these women actually conceived somewhat later than they thought. These people refuse to believe that nature would allow pregnancy to go on so long beyond the usual length of time.

There is no unquestioned record of the longest time a human can carry a living pregnancy, but there is no doubt that it can go three and four weeks beyond the normal time *without* any error in calculation. This is known as postmaturity.

However, 80 per cent of all women deliver within ten days before or after the calculated date of delivery.

WHAT THE MOTHER EXPERIENCES

(The symptoms and discomforts that are mentioned here are discussed fully in the chapters that follow.)

Your first three months. It is during the first three months of pregnancy that nausea (sometimes called morning sickness, though it can also occur any time of the day or night) is most frequent. Nausea usually abates after the third month; in many cases before then. But some women must endure nausea throughout pregnancy. For others, nausea may disappear early in pregnancy—only to occur again later.

The first bodily change of which you will be aware is likely to be a sense of fullness of the breasts. This feeling may begin before the time of your first missed period. At first this sense of fullness of the breasts is about the same degree as what you felt before your periods. But as the days go by, the breasts become more and more sensitive. In time you will notice a definite enlargement. How much bigger the breasts become, and when this enlargement becomes apparent, varies from woman to woman.

In the first weeks of pregnancy a change of which you are not aware is taking place in your uterus. If you are examined after your period has been delayed a week or more, your doctor will notice a bluish discoloration of that portion of your womb that projects into the vagina: the cervix. And he will find a definite softening. Your uterus will not show appreciable enlargement for at least two or three weeks.

Pregnancy of less than two months' duration can be detected only by internal examination—unless you resort to laboratory tests. But between the middle and the end of your third month your uterus reaches such a size that it may be felt on abdominal examination. By the end of your third month your obstetrician can feel your pregnant uterus from the outside simply by applying moderately firm pressure with his hand against your bladder region, just above the pubic bone.

Exactly when and how easily the enlargement of your uterus can be felt externally depends upon your size. If you are thin, your growing uterus can be felt earlier. If you are unusually obese, it cannot be felt till later. If your uterus lies in a normal position, toward the front of your abdomen, it can be much more easily felt than if it is "tipped" and lies toward your rectum.

If your uterus is "tipped" at the beginning of pregnancy, it must come forward by the end of your third month, for the hollow formed by your spinal column cannot contain a uterus of greater than three-month size, without causing tremendous pressure which interferes with bladder function. In practically all cases the uterus does come forward by the end of the third month without any manipulation being necessary.

If there is some delay, your obstetrician may instruct you to assume the knee-chest position (see Figure F, page 229) for short periods each day to encourage the uterus to fall forward. This position consists of kneeling on some comfortable surface like your bed, and at the same time resting your chest on the same surface, so that your buttocks become the highest part of your body and you are completely supported by your chest and knees. Only in cases where there is some definite abnormality, some adhesions binding the uterus in a "tipped" position, will it fail to assume its proper place by the beginning of the fourth month of pregnancy.

Your middle three months. The middle three months of pregnancy are usually the most comfortable. You will be over the worst of your nausea and at this stage will be suffering no real discomfort from the size or activity of your baby. You may "never have felt better" in your life. This is often reflected in your appearance. Many women are at their most beautiful during this stage of pregnancy.

By the end of your fourth month there is a slight but definite protrustion below your naval. And it is some time between now and the middle of your fifth month that you will first become aware of some little movements of your baby. This is popularly known as "feeling life," or "quickening."

By this time changes in skin pigmentation will be noticeable, especially in brunettes. The nipples and the circle of roughened skin about them, the *areola*, become darkened. A brown vertical line appears on the abdomen, below, and sometimes above the navel. It is called the *linea nigra*.

At about five months the protrusion caused by the growing baby inside you reaches the height of your navel. This is not an absolute rule, since the height of the navel varies on different women, and the amount of protrusion depends on your size. Small or thin women will show an earlier protrusion than taller or stouter women.

The greatest change in a woman's figure becomes apparent during the sixth month. It is at this time—betwen the end of the fifth and the end of the sixth month—that you suddenly begin to look pregnant. Now maternity clothes become a necessity rather than a proud boast. Before this the bulge is below your waistline, where a full skirt hides it. After this your waistline itself disappears.

At six months the top of the uterus has risen above the level of the navel. The movements of your baby have become much stronger.

Your last three months. During the last three months of pregnancy your baby's movements may sometimes become annoying. It may be extremely active a good deal of the time, kicking you under the ribs or low in the vagina. You will often be able to see your baby moving against your abdominal wall, sometimes causing a quite discernible bulge by pushing out some part of its body or limbs.

At seven months the top of your uterus rises to within three or four finger breadths of the lower end of your sternum, or breastbone.

After this, during the eighth and ninth months, there is just a general enlargement. Your uterus now tends to grow forward in the last two months, becoming more and more prominent—since it cannot expand upward indefinitely.

This outward expansion continues into the ninth month. Then, due to the expansion and development of the lower part of your uterus, the baby's head begins to find its way down lower, into the hollow portion of your pelvis. When this happens there suddenly seems to be less pressure against your ribs. You feel as though the burden that you have been carrying has actually become lighter. This is commonly called "lightening."

The feeling of lightening is probably *not entirely a mechanical one,* caused solely by the changing position of your baby. At this time, toward the last half of the ninth month, certain of the bodily changes associated with pregnancy begin to regress. The load upon your circulation and the amount of your body fluid begin to diminish. You feel less of a heaviness in breathing, your heartbeat becomes easier, and all in all the effort involved in ordinary movement grows less. You are about to become a mother.

WHERE YOUR BABY GROWS

The womb. During pregnancy, your baby lives and grows inside your uterus, which is also called the womb. As your baby grows from a tiny cluster of cells to a full-size infant ready for birth, your uterus, which is originally the size of a flattened pear, expands to accommodate it.

While inside your womb, your baby lives within a fluid-filled sac known as the "bag of waters." It gets its food and oxygen from your blood stream through the placenta (afterbirth), which connects the growing baby to the lining of your uterus.

The "bag of waters." The baby, during its development in the womb, is surrounded by two layers of membrane. The outer layer is called the chorion, and the placenta is part of this layer. There is also an inner layer, called the amnion. This is filled with a watery fluid called amniotic fluid. Your baby actually floats in this fluid throughout its development.

The fluid serves as a cushion, for one thing. Being incompressible, it protects the baby against shocks and falls. There must be damage to the uterus itself or a rupture of the bag of waters before there is any great likelihood of injury to your baby from any accident that you might have.

If your bag of waters ruptures at any stage of pregnancy, labor is very likely to follow within a few days. When the water bag does break, women are frequently astonished at the quantity of water that will escape, and the fact that it will continue to trickle out for days if the labor does not begin. The reason for this is that there is not simply a certain fixed amount of fluid within this sac. More fluid is constantly being produced, but as long as the sac is intact the fluid is reabsorbed at a balanced rate.

The placenta. The placenta (afterbirth) is actually a part of your baby. During the first multiplications of the cluster of cells formed after the fertilization of the egg, a tiny ball is formed that burrows into the wall of the uterus to obtain nourishment from your blood vessels. Later on a portion of this cluster of cells becomes specialized to form an organ known as the placenta. Its function is to nourish the growing embryo.

The rest of the embryo develops separately and is connected to the placenta by the umbilical cord, which is composed of a gelatinous substance and contains an artery and veins.

The placenta remains attached to the lining of the uterus. It develops a rich network of blood vessels that end in fine capillaries in little projections called villi. These projections actually invade your blood vessels and float about in the current of your blood. There is no direct mingling of the blood of the mother and that of the baby. But most of the substances dissolved in your blood are capable of passing through the walls of these tiny capillaries and entering the blood of the growing baby.

In the same way, waste products formed within the body of the growing embryo are carried by blood vessels into the placenta and passed through into the blood stream of the mother. They are eliminated through your kidneys and lungs.

The name "afterbirth" has been given to the placenta because in all normal cases it remains behind after the baby is born. Separation of the placenta takes place later—sometimes as early as a few seconds, usually several minutes, rarely hours. Further contractions of the uterus, which may be felt as mild additional labor pains, force the afterbirth out of the uterus into the vagina. Once again the woman is given the sensation of wishing to bear down to expel something. She then expels this mass of tissue, weighing approximately a pound. Hence the name: "afterbirth."

The question of what substances are capable of crossing this placental barrier between mother and unborn child is not entirely settled. Most of the simpler substances in the blood—sugar, nitrogenous waste products, salts—will pass through this barrier quite freely. The antibodies that confer immunity against disease also pass across this barrier from the mother to the infant. It is for this reason that if a mother is immune to such diseases as measles, smallpox, chicken pox, the baby will be born with an immunity also—an immunity that will persist for several months, or as long as these antibodies remain in the infant's circulation.

Drugs pass freely across the placental barrier in both directions. If the mother takes a sleeping pill, the baby also receives a proportionate dose. But just as it is eliminated from the mother's circulation by the action of her kidneys, liver, and so forth, so the baby's circulation is also cleared of the substance. It is filtered out of the baby's blood into the mother's, and taken care of by her organs of execretion.

In view of this ability of drugs to pass through the placenta into the infant's circulation, the question naturally arises as to whether any of them are likely to injure the baby. With rare exceptions, the answer is *no*. As long as the dose is safe for the mother—whether it be aspirin, sleeping pills, sulfa, penicillin, or other antibiotics—it will be harmless to the baby.

A possible exception is quinine, which has toxic effects on the auditory nerve and has been blamed for deafness in babies. The only other drugs that would be definitely harmful are of no importance to the expectant mother, since they are powerful poisons for all rapidly growing cells and are used only for treating cancer.

Addiction to narcotics *can* make an addict of the baby. Babies born of morphine addicts must be watched closely for convulsions due to being suddenly deprived of morphine, to which their nervous systems have grown accustomed while in the womb.

This, however, has nothing to do with the nightly use of barbiturates or other sleeping pills. Even though marked "caution—may be habit-forming," it is doubtful whether they cause true addiction in the adult, and certain that they do not in the infant. It has been claimed that infants are more likely to be problem sleepers if the mothers habitually used sleeping pills during pregnancy. If this is true, it is most likely the result of the mothers' nervous temperament, inherited or acquired.

Any *serious* infection in the mother is a threat to the unborn child. Even though bacteria do not ordinarily cross the placental barrier, the toxins they produce may.

Some viruses are known to have crossed the placenta, affecting the unborn child. The outstanding example is German measles which causes a high percentage of fetal abnormalities in the first 3 months. There has been some evidence implicating other viruses but no clear proof.

HOW YOUR BABY GROWS

First month. Early in the first month of pregnancy your fertilized egg rapidly undergoes many cell divisions, forming a tiny cluster of cells known as an embryo. Some of the cells in this cluster form your placenta, others develop into the bag of waters. The rest of the embryo cells are already at work forming your baby.

By the time you miss your first period, your baby's head and brain have already begun to take form. The head will continue to be the fastest-growing portion of the embryo and will be the largest part of the baby at birth.

By the end of the embryo's first month of life the rudimentary development of all your baby's internal organs has begun. The heart, though only a tiny tube at this stage, has already begun to beat. The backbone has begun to develop— and there is a definite tail at the end of it. Four tiny buds have appeared. These will grow into your baby's arms and legs.

At the end of this first month the embryo baby is about one sixth to one quarter of an inch in length, and is curled in a tight semicircle.

Second month. Your baby's arms and legs develop, complete with elbows, knees, and webbed fingers and toes. The tail becomes completely formed and reaches its greatest length. The lungs, heart, stomach, liver, and intestines begin to take the position they will occupy in the full-grown baby. Your baby's face, too, begins to acquire its features, including eye sockets, eyelids, and ears.

It is fascinating to realize how incredibly small all these features, limbs, and organs are at this stage. For your baby is only a bit more than an inch long and weighs less than one tenth of an ounce.

By the end of this second month the placenta is fully developed and the baby is immersed inside the bag of waters.

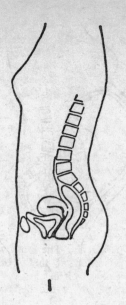 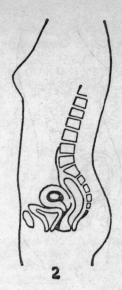

FIGURE C. How Your Baby Grows Inside You

1. Before pregnancy
2. At about one month

From now on, for the duration of pregnancy, the baby is referred to by medical men as the fetus.

Third month. Your baby's tail begins to diminish in size; by the end of the month it disappears. The webbing between the fingers and toes also disappears. Very thin fingernails and toenails appear, and the buds that will grow into baby teeth are forming in the gums.

Although the baby weighs only an ounce or less at the end of this month, the external sex organs are already visible. By the end of the third month, if this baby is a girl, she will already have a definite womb.

Fourth month. Your baby is growing rapidly. By the end of this month it will be four to six inches long and weigh about four ounces. It now looks like a baby, completely formed but with a great deal of growing to do. At this stage you could hold your baby cupped in the palm of your hand.

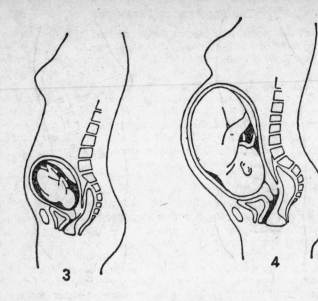

3. At six months   4. Full term, the baby ready to be born

Hair has begun to grow on the baby's head and fuzz appears on its body. At the end of the month, the baby's muscles become active and your baby begins to stir a little, stretching its arms and legs. These movements are slight as yet, but some women will notice them.

Fifth month. It is during this month that your baby begins to be so active that you can definitely feel it moving around inside you. It is also during this month that your doctor may first be able to hear the baby's heart beat with the aid of a stethoscope.

Your baby is now growing large enough to make a noticeable bulge in your abdomen.

Sixth month. As the expansion of your abdomen indicates, your baby increases in size and weight quite markedly through this and the remaining months of pregnancy. By the end of this month your baby is about one foot "tall" and may weigh more than one-and-a-half pounds.

Your baby is doing more than stretching now—as you can probably feel, perhaps somewhat painfully. It kicks and bobs its head, moves its whole body to change position within you. It turns from side to side, sometimes "sits" and other times "stands on its head." This movement and thrashing about continue for the duration of pregnancy, but they are not usually constant. There will probably be times when you feel no movement at all. Babies seem to have periods of sleep and wakefulness while inside you.

Seventh month. The internal organs of your baby are nearing their full development, and in some cases are now capable of functioning outside the mother. Babies born toward the end of this month have a chance to survive under prompt medical care.

During this month the baby usually settles into the position in which it will be delivered—whether the head-down position, or, more rarely, a feet-first position, or, still more rarely, a horizontal position. But this position may change any time up to birth. The baby continues to move in other ways: thrashing its arms and legs, jerking its head about, turning so that its buttocks are sometimes toward your navel, other times toward your spine.

Eighth month. Your baby is beginning to acquire its baby fat, weighing in the neighborhood of four pounds. Babies born during the eighth month have a good chance to survive.

Ninth month. A growth of fine hair covers the baby's head, while most of the downy fuzz has disappeared from its body. Your baby fills out rapidly during this last month. At birth, the average baby weighs between six and one half and seven pounds and is about twenty inches long; but individual babies may vary: Under five and one half pounds is considered premature, and over eight and three quarters pounds is classified as excessive size.

If your baby is born at any time after the end of the eighth month, its chance to live is as good as that of a baby that is born after the full nine months.

If you have twins. The presence of twins is not diagnosed during pregnancy unless it is thought about. In the clinic services, in the best hospitals, diagnosis is made in little more than half the cases before actual birth. But in private practice, where you are more closely observed—and by the same observer on each visit—your doctor is more likely to be aware that your abdomen is increasing in size more rapidly than normal.

As early as the fourth month your obstetrician may note that your pregnancy seems at least a month farther advanced than the dates would warrant—and yet you feel no life and he can hear no heartbeat. This may be due to factors other than a twin pregnancy: Excessive accumulation of fluid, a large baby, occasionally just your build may make you appear to have enlarged more rapidly.

The obstetrician who suspects a twin pregnancy will usually keep his suspicions to himself until he can be more certain—unless you yourself suspect twins and ask him about it. The fetal skeleton is not sufficiently calcified to show up distinctly in an X ray before the sixth month of pregnancy. Rarely will an X ray be taken at this stage simply to verify the presence of twins, since no special treatment is called for.

By the seventh or eighth month it is possible to suspect, by feeling the abdomen, that there is more than one baby. At this time it may also be possible to distinguish more than one fetal heartbeat.

MISCARRIAGES

The tendency to miscarry. On their first visit to their obstetrician, women are naturally concerned about the possibility that they may miscarry. They are anxious to know what they can do to prevent a miscarriage—whether they should abstain from physical activity, travel, and so forth.

About 10 per cent of all pregnancies do terminate in miscarriages—the greater number of these miscarriages occurring during the first three months of pregnancy. But if a miscarriage does occur, it is rarely the result of anything a woman has done or has failed to do. The popular tendency is to blame some overstrenuous activity such as travel, sexual intercourse, a fall. But there are very few cases for which anything of this sort is responsible.

Miscarriages are generally caused by some genetic failure or a failure of the fertilized egg to implant properly. This occurs in the first weeks of pregnancy. By the time staining appears, the ovum may have been dead for days or weeks.

Staining alone, however, is not a sure sign of impending

miscarriage. As was explained in the section on conception, about 25 per cent of all women stain sometime during the first three months of pregnancy. Staining is always a reason for immediately calling your obstetrician. But two thirds of the women who stain will carry on the pregnancy without any special treatment.

One common fear that should be laid to rest is that if a woman stains or bleeds during a pregnancy she *should* miscarry—that if she has such staining and doesn't miscarry, the baby born of the pregnancy may be abnormal. There is absolutely no truth to this belief. Nor is there any truth to the belief that if a woman miscarries, and then has a full-term pregnancy the next time, the child born of this subsequent pregnancy may be abnormal. It just isn't so.

Repeated early miscarriages. When miscarriage occurs early (that is, in the first three months of pregnancy) a woman has as good a chance of having a successful pregnancy the next time as any woman who has never had a miscarriage—providing no organic disease or congenital defect is responsible.

Some medical men have said that if a woman has one miscarriage, her chances of the next pregnancy carrying through successfully are 85 to 90 per cent. That if she has two consecutive miscarriages, her chances the next time are about 50-50. That if she has three consecutive miscarriages, the chances that she will carry through her next pregnancy drop to only about 15 per cent. In other words, these men believe that all such women have a tendency to habitual miscarriage.

My personal view is that this reasoning is not sound. It tends to be disproved by the very statistics released by the various groups experimenting with treatments of so-called habitual miscarriages. Whatever the treatment used—whether stilbesterol or orange juice—all of these groups managed to achieve about an 85-per-cent cure rate. That is, 85 per cent of the women who miscarried and then took treatments carried through their next pregnancy successfully. This happens to be the same rate as for *any* woman who becomes pregnant. Whether she's miscarried before or not, she has an 85 to 90 per cent chance of carrying through successfully.

Repeated early miscarriages may be the result of the workings of the law of chance, rather than the result of any specific disease or abnormality. Based on pure chance, the odds are about one thousand to one against your having three miscarriages in a row. But since the numbers of pregnancies each year run into the hundreds of thousands, even the thousand-to-one chance is bound to find its victims.

In denying that three consecutive miscarriages is proof of a tendency to habitual miscarriage, I do not wish to deny that such a tendency ever exists. I merely wish to urge caution in concluding that any treatment under which such a woman succeeds in carrying a pregnancy has thereby demonstrated its value.

Certainly any woman who has had three consecutive miscarriages should undergo the most painstaking investigation to rule out disease, developmental defects, or glandular disturbances. And since the outcome of pregnancy may be determined during the first days of implantation, before the period is missed, treatment may have to begin each month even before the woman is sure that she has conceived.

Repeated late miscarriages. Any woman may have one miscarriage late in pregnancy and then carry through her next pregnancy normally. But there are a number of unfortunate women who have a tendency to repeated late miscarriages.

In some cases this is associated with kidney trouble or high blood pressure. Such patients should not risk further pregnancies.

A few years ago an Indian gynecologist, Dr. Shirodkar, demonstrated that some women had a condition called "cervical incompetence" which caused late miscarriages. In these women the cervix dilates almost painlessly during the middle three months of pregnancy with no sign other than perhaps a pinkish mucus discharge. When the doctor examines the patient he finds the bag of waters bulging into the vagina. As soon as it ruptures the fetus is born.

This condition is due to a deficiency of the circular band of muscle which normally keeps the lower part of the uterus closed until labor takes place. It is detected in the nonpregnant woman by a special X-ray technique, placing a balloon in the uterus.

Various operations have been devised to correct this condition. Generally they involve encircling the cervix with a nonabsorbable suture, as a draw string might close a purse held upside down.

The operation is not 100% successful. When performed

during pregnancy, miscarriage may follow immediately. When performed after pregnancy, there may be difficulty conceiving.

When the operation is successful and the patient subsequently goes into labor, her obstetrician will decide whether the suture should be cut for normal delivery, or whether she should be delivered by Caesarean section.

Signs and symptoms of threatened miscarriage. "Miscarriage" is not strictly a medical term. The technical term is "abortion," which in the minds of laymen is usually reserved for intentional interruption of pregnancy. However, it carries no such significance medically.

Miscarriage during the first three months of pregnancy is referred to as early abortion. It usually follows vaginal bleeding and cramps.

During the middle three months it may be referred to as late abortion—and the symptoms that usher it in are the same as those symptoms which occur early in pregnancy. With one addition. Without any special warning the bag of waters may rupture. There is a gush of fluid, sometimes followed by a little stain, sometimes not. In these cases, miscarriage will usually take place within a few days to a week—except in rare cases where the leak has taken place high up in the uterus and seems to heal spontaneously.

As pregnancy advances and we approach the time when there is a chance that the baby, though immature, may survive, the term abortion—or miscarriage—is no longer used. Termination of pregnancy is now referred to as "premature labor." This again may be ushered in by the appearance of a stain, or cramps; a sudden mucus discharge or loss of water.

Any case where there is vaginal bleeding or cramps may be considered *threatened* miscarriage. If there is a *combination* of definite cramps and bleeding, miscarriage is usually inevitable.

Bleeding and cramps not followed by miscarriage. Vaginal bleeding at any time during the early months of pregnancy must be considered as a sign of possible impending miscarriage. But, as was explained elsewhere, about 25 per cent of all pregnant women have some degree of vaginal bleeding during the first three months of pregnancy. Sometimes this bleeding will appear at about the time of the first or second missed period, but this does not give it greater or lesser significance. If this staining is of relatively short duration—

ending within a few days—if it is less in amount than a normal period and is not associated with cramps, the chances of the pregnancy continuing to a normal birth are good.

In some cases the flow may be heavier than is normally experienced during a menstrual period—on account of rupture of some vessel near the margin of the advancing placenta. This might cause an alarming gush of blood, which ceases fairly abruptly and is followed by a *moderate* amount of brown staining for a few days. The pregnancy usually continues uneventfully from that point on.

Cramps, occurring without any vaginal bleeding, need not be considered a cause for alarm in early pregnancy.

How a miscarriage occurs. When vaginal staining *persists,* even if it is not so heavy as menstrual bleeding—when it is dark red one day, then brown, then recurring red—it is an ominous sign, even if no cramps have developed. There may be an abrupt disappearance of symptoms of pregnancy. Nausea suddenly diminishes; the breasts become less sensitive and appear smaller. Such signs, in conjunction with bleeding, indicate that the ovum has already perished and it is just a question of time until it is expelled.

In some cases there may be a *very slight* staining, but rather severe menstrual-like cramps. It is much more difficult to be certain of the death of the egg in such cases, since it is not possible to identify with absolute certainty the source of the cramps. They could be intestinal rather than uterine in origin.

Following a period of staining, a woman may feel a chilly, grippy, ill feeling, sometimes accompanied by a sudden wave of nausea and vomiting. This, having followed a period of staining with signs that the uterus has not developed so rapidly as normal (which can only be determined by the doctor), is due to toxic absorption of the dead products. Under these circumstances, miscarriage will probably take place shortly.

The actual emptying of the uterus is the final act of the miscarriage. This is ushered in by cramps of varying severity. They may be similar to those which a woman experienced with menstruation. Or they may approach in intensity the pains of labor. These cramps may persist for a varying length of time, accompanied by increased vaginal bleeding and passage of large clots. During this time the cervix (the neck of the womb) dilates just as it would in labor—only to a miniature extent. Eventually the ovum is expelled from the uterus and discharged from the vagina.

Curettage. When the uterus promptly and completely empties itself, very little treatment is required. But if the bleeding has been severe, or the pain strong enough to warrant hospitalization, most obstetricians feel that the wisest course is to make sure that the uterus is empty by performing a minor operation known as a curettage.

This must be done under anesthesia. It consists of exposing the opening into the womb as one would during an examination and gently scraping the lining of the uterus to make sure that remaining bits of afterbirth are removed. (A small amount of tissue remaining in the uterus may cause fever or recurrent bleeding for weeks.) There is no cutting involved in this operation. And there is no discomfort following it. The woman is up and about the next day.

When the bleeding has never been alarming in amount and the pains have not been severe, the dead ovum is frequently expelled at home. The obstetrician may wait to see whether the evidence points to a complete spontaneous emptying of the uterus. If bleeding diminishes to a mere stain within a week, becoming progressively less, it is not necessary for the woman to be taken to the hospital for the operation of curettage.

"Missed abortion." A woman may have cramps, staining, and evidence that her pregnancy is no longer thriving (the uterus stops growing, the breasts become soft, and all symptoms of pregnancy disappear) yet not have a miscarriage. The embryo has perished in the uterus, but there is no sign that the uterus is actively attempting to expel the dead products of conception.

The course of action followed depends on how far the pregnancy has advanced. If there is little bleeding, and the pregnancy is three or four months along, the wisest course agreed upon by all obstetricians is to wait. There is no danger that the woman will become infected or "poisoned" by the dead tissue within her—if simple hygienic precautions are taken. It is, of course, an unpleasant situation for the woman. She wishes to be rid of a pregnancy that is no longer thriving as soon as possible. But it can only cause complications to attempt to empty her uterus prematurely. Usually the time will come when the uterus will spontaneously empty itself.

Treatment of threatened miscarriage. It is practically universally agreed that at the first sign of a possible miscarriage complete rest is indicated. It is customary to get into bed immediately and stay there as long as any sign of staining continues.

It is difficult to evaluate scientifically how important rest or any particular medication may be in preventing a miscarriage after signs of one have developed. Every obstetrician sees in his practice working girls and mothers with small children to take care of who continue their usual activities in spite of staining. A large percentage of these women carry through their pregnancies and have normal full-term babies.

However, it is impossible to study a comparable series of cases to evaluate the effect of exercise on miscarriage. Women decide for themselves how much activity they will indulge in —depending more on how anxious they are to preserve the pregnancy than upon the instructions of their doctors.

Tradition is probably more important than science in influencing the conduct of women who show signs of threatened miscarriage. Certainly, the woman who has had difficulty in conceiving or carrying will want to have a completely clear conscience regardless of the outcome. She will undertake no activity that might possibly encourage a miscarriage.

All sex activity should definitely be avoided the minute any sign of threatened miscarriage appears. Intercourse may introduce infection in the presence of blood and, possibly, dead tissue in the uterus. And sexual stimulation of any type can stimulate stronger contractions of the uterus. If the uterus is already in an irritable state, this may encourage loosening and ejection of the embryo.

Medication. Over the years a great variety of medications, hormones, and vitamins have held first place in the treatment of threatened abortion. It has been very difficult to find scientific proof that any one of them is consistently effective.

In a third of the cases, by the time any bleeding appears the embryo is already perishing or defective; no treatment can possibly be effective. And in the other two thirds of the cases probably no treatment is necessary. The bleeding is merely a leakage of blood from the advancing placenta as it invades the lining of the uterus. Medication can probably help only in a small percentage of cases, where some organic defect or nutritive lack is threatening the life of the embryo.

At one time vitamin E was held to be the answer, because it was shown that in rats on a diet deficient in vitamin E pregnancy could not be carried through; the embryo died in the uterus and was reabsorbed. However, it would be very difficult to devise a diet for a human that will not contain considerable quantities of vitamin E. It would appear unlikely that vitamin E deficiency plays an important part in causing miscarriages.

The hormone progesterone held a high place for a time. It was shown in animals that, in early pregnancy, if the corpus luteum in the ovary (the source of progesterone) were removed, miscarriage took place. However, this sort of reasoning does not prove that miscarriage in the human is due to lack of progesterone. Shortly after its discovery, very small quantities of progesterone were used, because it was too expensive to give larger amounts. These infinitely small quantities were given credit for saving large numbers of pregnancies. Today, when more reasonable doses are economically possible, there are probably some cases in which progesterone has saved pregnancies. Studies have indicated a low rate of progesterone formation among *some* women who subsequently miscarried. For these women, treatment with progesterone might have prevented miscarriage.

In recent years hormones have been produced which have powerful progesterone effects when taken by mouth. These are used in threatened abortion, and one of them is becoming even more popular as the "birth control pill."

Stilbesterol—a powerful synthetic estrogenic hormone—has enjoyed the greatest vogue for preventing miscarriage. This is due to the fact that it is relatively cheap, and effective when taken by mouth, so that impressive doses may be given. The theory behind its administration is that it stimulates production of progesterone by the placenta. The wave of enthusiasm that greeted first reports of success appears to be diminishing. About all that has been proved beyond question is that fantastic amounts may be given without apparent harm.

Lately a form of vitamin C, with an added factor known as "flavonoids," has been advised for preventing miscarriage, because it has been shown to strengthen capillaries and prevent bleeding. But this means that it should be effective only where increased fragility of capillaries is a factor in causing a threatened miscarriage.

In summary, no one medication can be the answer to the problem of miscarriage any more than any one drug can be expected to cure all fevers. Until the science of bacteriology revealed the specific germ causing each type of fever, it was the custom to treat them all with quinine, since this medicine was notably successful against malaria, killing the then-unknown malarial parasite. Today we stand almost in the same position in the treatment of threatened miscarriage.

It is quite possible that stilbesterol is effective in preventing miscarriage due to one cause, and progesterone, vitamin E, citrus flavonoids, etc., in preventing miscarriage due to other causes. But methods of demonstrating specific causes for each individual case are not yet available, so we grope in the dark, trying whatever may possibly do good and cannot possibly do harm.

Psychological factors. Under severe emotional disturbance, a person's face may blanch and turn fiery red, the blood supply may drain away from the brain—causing a person to faint. So, too, the blood supply to the uterus may be sufficiently disturbed by emotional shock to bring on strong contractions and separate the placenta from the lining—causing bleeding, cramps, and miscarriage.

Whether chronic anxiety or long-sustained but less severe emotional disturbance can have a similar effect it is difficult to prove. Certainly there is some evidence that reassurance has benefited women who have suffered repeated miscarriages.

RH FACTOR

Rh problems are not common. The only reason for devoting more than a paragraph or two to the Rh factor is the amount of scare-story publicity it has received. Because of this publicity, most women are worried about it. Actually, the possibility of you or your child suffering because of the Rh factor is very, very slight—even if you are Rh negative and your husband is Rh positive.

Rh troubles from transfusions. There are four major types of blood. These blood types are AB, A, B, and O. The Rh factor is one of the minor blood types. It was first discovered around 1940. About 85 per cent of all people have this factor in their red blood cells; these people are known as Rh positive. The other 15 per cent do not have this factor in their blood, and are known as Rh negative.

Before this subgroup was discovered, if a woman received a blood transfusion all that was known about her blood was whether she should be given type AB, A, B, or O blood. Whichever of these types she was given, the chances were six to one that the blood given to her would be Rh positive. If this woman were an Rh negative, the Rh positive cells in the transfused blood that she had received would act like a foreign protein. Her system would begin to produce antibodies to fight this Rh invader.

If this woman subsequently became pregnant by an Rh positive husband, and her child inherited her husband's Rh positive type of blood, these antibodies in her system could pass through her placenta and enter her baby's circulation. This would result in injury to her baby's blood cells and its blood-forming organs, producing a condition known as erythroblastosis.

Varying amounts of damage may be done to the baby, depending on the amount of these antibodies and how early they appear. In some cases, the damage is so extensive that the baby dies unborn. In other cases the baby is delivered with varying degrees of jaundice or damage to the brain and central nervous system. Still others, born with no evidence of disease, have antibodies in their blood and rapidly develop jaundice and anemia unless treated.

Fortunately, women having babies today have grown up largely in the period since the Rh factor was discovered. Therefore, they are much less likely to have received a transfusion of the wrong type blood.

But while the cause of the most serious type of Rh factor trouble in an Rh negative woman is receiving a transfusion of Rh positive blood, there is another cause—though less frequent: Rh trouble because of repeated pregnancies alone. If you are Rh positive, or if you are Rh negative and your husband is also Rh negative, you have nothing to worry about. It is when you are Rh negative and your husband is Rh positive that trouble may *sometimes* occur.

If you are Rh negative and your husband is Rh positive. In this case your baby will probably also be Rh positive— since the positive factor is dominant. Apparently there is some leakage of an infant's blood cells into the mother's circulation. So that if you are Rh negative, and have repeated pregnancies with Rh positive babies, in time you *may* become sensitized enough so that your blood will contain large quantities of antibodies. Once this occurs you will have trouble in any subsequent pregnancy as long as the embryo is Rh positive.

But you should not be too alarmed about this possibility, even if you are Rh negative and your husband is Rh positive. First of all, there is practically no chance that your first child will be in any way affected. And there is little chance that your second or even your third child will, because only a small percentage of Rh negative women will become sensitized simply by being pregnant and carrying Rh positive babies.

Secondly, in spite of the fact that the positive factor is dominant, not all Rh positive men produce only Rh positive babies. For there are two types of Rh positive men. These types are known as homozygous and heterozygous.

A homozygous husband will always have Rh positive babies, even when his wife is Rh negative. This is not true of the heterozygous husband. Half of his sperm carry the factor that will make his offspring Rh positive; but the other half of his sperm do not, so that there is a 50-50 chance the offspring would be Rh negative if the mother were Rh negative.

As long as the husband is heterozygous, an Rh negative woman need not despair—even if she has had one child with Rh trouble and has a large quantity of antibodies in her blood. There is still the same 50-50 chance that their next baby will be Rh negative. This child will not be affected by the antibodies.

In severe cases, if a woman has developed antibodies in her blood—whether from a transfusion or through pregnancy—her doctor will discourage her from having more babies, unless there is a chance that they will be Rh negative. It is possible that after a number of years her antibody level will drop low enough so that she can take a chance with another pregnancy. However, once the body has responded to any foreign protein with antibody formations, it usually responds very quickly again. So there is only the slightest chance that a woman once sensitized would be able to bear a perfectly healthy Rh positive baby.

I must state again that the danger of such trouble from the Rh factor is small—especially in first pregnancies or in any pregnancy in which the mother shows no anti-Rh antibodies at the beginning of the pregnancy. And when these antibodies appear later, there are now methods of dealing with the situation.

Dealing with Rh factor trouble. Now that the Rh factor is known, methods have been devised for dealing with trouble that it may cause. Babies who are born with the antibodies in their blood can now be saved—and will grow up perfectly healthy.

On one of your first visits to your obstetrician he will test your blood for the Rh factor. If he finds that you are Rh negative, he will test your husband's blood. If your husband has Rh positive blood, your obstetrician will test your blood again as pregnancy progresses—particularly in the last months—to see whether you have developed antibodies. Should he find that a large quantity of antibodies are developing in your blood, he will prepare to deal with the situation. What he does will be the same whether these antibodies develop because of past pregnancies, or because you previously received a transfusion of Rh positive blood.

At one time it was felt that if the antibody level in the mother was rising during pregnancy, the best solution was to deliver the baby as early as possible. A Caesarean was done as soon as the baby was large enough to survive, so that it would not be exposed to further harmful effects from the mother's antibodies. But it was found that the premature babies were the most susceptible to such damage, and their survival rate was poor. Today, early induction of labor or premature Caesarean is not felt to be the solution.

Instead, if the obstetrician sees that the antibody level in the mother is rising to a dangerous degree, he will alert a blood-transfusion specialist to be on hand with Rh negative blood when the baby is delivered.

If the baby is born with jaundice or any other symptoms caused by antibodies, or if a test known as the Coombs Test reveals that the baby's blood cells have been sensitized by its mother's antibodies, the baby is immediately subjected to exchange transfusions. Blood is removed from the baby and replaced with Rh negative blood. Then there is further blood removed and more replacement by transfusion. So that, by degrees, there is a change of about 80 per cent of the infant's blood.

The transfused Rh negative blood is immune to the anti-Rh antibodies produced by the mother. This transfused blood will remain in the baby's circulation until the antibodies are gradually eliminated. Then the Rh positive blood cells produced by the baby itself are able to survive.

A word on jaundiced babies. It is possible for an Rh negative woman to give birth to a child who subsequently develops a yellow jaundice which is *not* due to any effect of the Rh factor. A large percentage of perfectly normal babies will show some degree of jaundice for reasons that are not entirely understood. This is known as physiological jaundice. It usually appears about the second, third, or fourth day of life. Sometimes it becomes quite deep. Usually it clears by the sixth or seventh day.

In addition, there are cases where an Rh negative woman is type O and her baby inherits the type A blood. Even if the mother is negative and her baby is positive, she may develop no anti-Rh antibodies. Instead, her blood may produce anti-A antibodies, which will cause a mild condition resembling Rh factor trouble. Rarely serious, this condition practically never requires an exchange transfusion— although in the cases where there is pronounced anemia, the baby may need a transfusion of additional blood.

So, if an Rh negative woman and her Rh positive husband have a child who develops jaundice, the Rh factor is not necessarily responsible. If the Rh factor was not the cause of the jaundice, there is no reason why this couple should not have more children.

CHAPTER 8

Pregnancy Do's and Don'ts

PHYSICAL ACTIVITY

Everything in moderation. Your chief guide when it comes to physical activity during pregnancy—whether it is sports, sex, or work—is: Everything in moderation. How much you do should depend on how you feel. Don't push yourself to the point of exhaustion. If you feel any discomfort, stop what you are doing for the time being.

Physical activity in itself is not a cause of miscarriage, except perhaps in rare cases where something rather violent is concerned. But when you are pregnant you are more easily fatigued. Fatigue can bring with it a train of symptoms. It accentuates every normal discomfort to which a pregnant woman may be subject, and can actually bring on depression and other symptoms of emotional disturbance.

If you feel tired, rest. You definitely require more rest when you are pregnant.

Exercise and sports. Mild exercise, which is not carried to the point of exhaustion, is healthful. It gives a feeling of toning up the body and generally improves your sense of well-being. It may possibly stimulate some of your bodily functions.

The less strenuous sports are also healthful, when indulged in only to the point of feeling *pleasantly* tired and relaxed. Though there is little proof of serious harm even from such sports as tennis, golf, and riding, the obstetrician would hardly recommend this sort of exercise. The fact that these sports are more fatiguing is not the only reason. For early in pregnancy there is relaxation of the ligament that binds the pubic bones together and closes in front the circle of bones that make up the pelvic girdle. This lengthening prepares the pelvis for greater expansion in case of need at the time of delivery of your child. But it also gives more play to the sacroiliac joint that binds the pelvic bones to the spine. Because of this greater mobility of this joint, sports that involve twisting, turning, sudden stops, and change of position are more likely to bring on severe back strain.

Swimming is permissible during pregnancy (but not diving, of course). Avoid violent surf and extremely cold water. The common-sense rules of safety that apply to all swimmers should be more stringently observed by the pregnant woman. For when you are pregnant you are more susceptible to dizziness, faintness, and muscle cramps. Don't swim alone and don't take chances. At the beach, remember that the sun can also be dangerous. Included among famous last words should be "I never burn. I tan."

Travel. This is the subject of much discussion. The traditional attitude against travel during pregnancy has been handed down from a time when travel meant something altogether different from what it means today. After all, fifty years ago travel was an ordeal of bouncing and lurching about in wagons and coaches—often without tires or springs—on unpaved roads. Certainly it was much more strenuous than traveling on modern highways or riding in today's trains and planes.

Some obstetricians still place limits on the *distances* a pregnant woman may travel. For prolonged travel, like overindulgence in sports, can be exhausting.

The only statistical study that has been made on the effects of travel on pregnancy was drawn from the experience with wives of men in the military services. It was found that women who did a considerable amount of traveling from one base to another during pregnancy had no higher miscarriage rate than those who stayed at home throughout pregnancy.

Working during pregnancy. A large percentage of the women an obstetrician sees today—especially in city practice—are working when they become pregnant for the first time. Some of them are financially able to leave their jobs, and are anxious to do so as promptly as possible to devote themselves to care of their home and preparations for the new arrival. Many others—for economic reasons, or simply because they enjoy their work—wish to continue working as long as they feel they will do no harm to themselves or their unborn child.

Should you go on working? Yes, if you want to. Most women maintain a healthier outlook throughout pregnancy if their way of life is not changed too abruptly. Unless your work entails some physical hazard, or some abnormal condition should arise in the pregnancy itself, there is no reason why you should stop.

Advice as to how long you should go on working after you become pregnant must naturally depend upon the type of work you do. But most women are employed in occupations requiring no great physical labor, the most arduous part of their job being the travel to and from work. It is difficult to see how office work could do harm even if continued into the ninth month. However, the majority of women will be content to stop working at a time when their pregnancy becomes quite obvious. This is usually between five and six months.

If you are going to work during pregnancy, you must realize that you will have to curtail your activities as a housewife to some extent. You will need some help with the more strenuous duties of housekeeping.

If you come home tired, make dinner that night from the simplest prepared foods. Or, if you can, eat out.

Keep entertaining to a minimum. If you are to go on with your job during pregnancy, you must use your weekends wisely—for rest and recuperation, rather than for social engagements involving late hours.

Sexual activity. Much conflicting advice has been given on this subject. Some people believe that the time when a woman would be having a period if she were not pregnant is a particularly vulnerable one. They believe that all strenuous activities, including intercourse, should be curtailed at these times.

Personally, I have never been convinced of the validity of this view. Few women have regular enough cycles to establish this "vulnerable time" with any accuracy by the time they have missed two or three periods.

The basis for this belief is probably the fact that staining may occur at times when a period is due during pregnancy. Since it is impossible to know when this is physiological, all staining must be regarded as a threat of miscarriage. If a woman stains or feels as though a period is coming on, she should take all precautions. But in the absence of such symptoms, she can safely ignore the calendar.

There are other theories that link sexual intercourse with miscarriage. Some doctors have advised that no woman should have intercourse during the first three months and last two months of pregnancy. Actually, I know of very little scientific evidence that intercourse is *ever* in itself a cause of miscarriage—unless carried on with unusual violence.

Sexual activity is permissible for most pregnant women as long as it is comfortable and pleasurable.

There is, however, one reservation, which does not apply to early pregnancy so much as to later pregnancy. For women who have shown some tendency to premature labor or miscarriage it may be well to keep all forms of sex stimulation to a minimum. This is because strong emotions of *any kind* seem to have the ability to stimulate uterine contractions. This can sometimes result in the threat of miscarriage.

This has been observed under many circumstances. The obstetrician at one army base, for example, noted that when a great number of orders for overseas duty came in, among the airmen's wives who were pregnant many more cases of vaginal bleeding and threatened miscarriage occurred. Women themselves will observe that if they become aroused by mental or physical stimulation the uterus will go into a strong and prolonged contraction.

CLOTHING

Girdles. There are women with good abdominal muscles who are perfectly comfortable without a girdle. They are not used to wearing one, and they can go through an entire pregnancy in comfort without one. If you are one of these women, there is no reason why you should be forced to wear a girdle during pregnancy.

There is no evidence that a girdle will help the skin as far as stretching is concerned, or that it will improve the quality of the abdominal muscles following delivery. The condition of your abdomen after delivery depends on the muscular development that you established before pregnancy. The amount of skin stretching depends on the amount of water in the uterus and the size of your baby or babies. A girdle will not alter this.

However, the majority of women are used to the sensation of a supporting girdle. If you are one of these women, you will require this support during pregnancy as you have before pregnancy.

Naturally, after four to five months of pregnancy, as your waistline begins to expand, the girdle that was snug before will become uncomfortably so. You will have to get an adjustable maternity girdle at this time.

Maternity girdles need not have any special orthopedic quality, unless you have some special weakness that requires treatment. Ordinarily, a maternity girdle need give no more support than the girdle you wore before pregnancy. A light, two-way-stretch maternity girdle is perfectly adequate. Don't worry about its being too tight. Your baby floats in water, which cannot be compressed. If the girdle is comfortable for you, it cannot be harming your child.

Brassières. There is usually no need for any special type of supporting brassière during pregnancy. As your breasts develop, a larger brassière becomes necessary. But unless discomfort from the increased size and weight of your breasts becomes a problem, no special support such as the crisscross type of brassière is called for. Such devices will not determine what sort of figure you will have after your pregnancy is over.

Shoes. I hesitate to express any opinion on women's fashions, but obviously their shoes were not primarily designed as an aid in walking. High heels, especially in conjunction with the popular backless shoes, give a woman a most unstable type of footing. On uneven ground particularly, if your ankle turns the slightest bit, high heels will increase the tendency to lose your balance and fall—or else to wrench your back severely in an effort to recover balance.

These possibilities are especially unpleasant when you are pregnant. A bad fall seems to occur at some time during nearly every pregnancy. In no case have I seen real harm result, but it is certainly a cause for anxiety, and to be avoided as much as possible. Even when you do not fall, you are very likely to strain your back in recovering your balance, for in pregnancy the sacroiliac joints in the back are more vulnerable than at other times.

However, you should not go into a much lower heel than

you are accustomed to wearing. When you have worn high heels for a long time, the large tendon in the calf of your leg has shortened. If you try to change suddenly into flat heels, it will cause a feeling of strain in the backs of your legs and behind your knees. The change in posture may also cause you backache.

For the average woman a medium heel is best. Also make sure that your shoes are firm enough, and the heels broad enough, to give you a surer tread and adequate support through a time when you will be gaining some twenty or more pounds.

Support for stockings. The one method of stocking support that you must absolutely not use during pregnancy is the round garters that constrict circulation in the legs. There is an increased blood supply to the pelvis during pregnancy, causing increased back pressure in the veins of your legs. These veins normally become more prominent. Any constriction that hampers the return flow of this increased amount of blood from your lower extremities may increase the tendency toward varicose veins.

If you wear a girdle, stocking support is no problem. If you do not wear a girdle, a maternity garter belt may be used. If this is not comfortable for you, there are special suspenders that go over the shoulders to support the stockings of pregnant women.

HYGIENE

Bathing. You can take showers throughout pregnancy. Tub bathing is also permitted during most of your pregnancy. But whether you are taking a shower or a bath, overheating may cause faintness, and sudden chilling may cause harmful reflex changes in your circulation.

For many years it has been the custom to forbid tub bathing in the last six weeks or month of pregnancy. It has been feared that infected material might get into the vagina and cause infection of the uterus at the time of delivery. Under modern hygienic conditions it is doubtful whether danger of infection is significantly increased by tub bathing.

Douching. Do not douche during your pregnancy—unless your obstetrician prescribes a douche for treatment of a specific condition and gives you careful instruction as to how it must be taken.

Care of breasts. Fairly early in pregnancy there may be a small amount of secretion from your nipples. This secretion is colostrum, the precursor of milk. It may form a crust particularly noticeable on rising in the morning. It is easily removed by washing. Your nipples and breasts require no special care except the cleanliness accorded the rest of your body. If you intend to breast-feed your baby, however, your doctor will give you instructions, during the final weeks of pregnancy, for preparing your nipples (see page 158).

Dental care. During pregnancy there is a general tendency to congestion of the tissues of your body. You may notice that your nose will sometimes become very stuffy because of this. And it is because of this, also, that your gums may become spongy and bleed on brushing.

There is a tendency to increased tooth decay during pregnancy. It is popular to blame this decay on the demands of the growing baby for calcium. This does *not* appear to be the reason. Any accelerated dental decay in pregnant women is probably caused by chemical and immunological changes that occur during pregnancy, plus the sponginess of the gums. Possibly the pregnancy hormones act on the secretions of your mouth in the same way as they act on the secretions of the vagina, causing conditions more favorable to the growth of lactic-acid-producing bacteria.

Because of this tendency toward gum sponginess and tooth decay, dental care is most important for every pregnant woman. If you have not had a thorough dental checkup very recently, you should see your dentist as early in pregnancy as possible.

If your dentist finds decay, or any troublesome condition, he should treat it. There is no form of dental work that cannot be carried out during pregnancy if the dentist feels it is necessary. This applies to the extraction of infected teeth. There is no reason why a pregnant woman should endure a toothache any more than one who is not pregnant.

The usual types of anesthesia are permissible during pregnancy—both the local injection of novocaine and inhalation of gas—provided you have no unusual reaction to the use of these agents when you are not pregnant.

X-rays. Publicity given to "fall-out" has caused exaggerated fears of X-rays. There is no question that a large enough dose of X-ray can produce disastrous effects on the developing embryo, and that the uterus and ovaries should be shielded if possible whenever exposure is necessary. But follow-up studies of thousands of cases have revealed no evidence of harm from X-rays used to study the shape of the pelvis and the position of the baby.

Diagnostic X-ray procedures to the abdominal area should be kept to a minimum. The amount of exposure from dental X-rays is negligible.

Smoking. There is no evidence that tobacco smoking by a pregnant woman has any injurious effect upon her unborn child. As far as the effects upon the woman herself are concerned, medical literature today is full of conflicting reports. However, no one is claiming that there are any *beneficial* effects to be had from smoking.

Smoke certainly is an irritant to the nasal passages. It causes some disturbances in digestion when indulged in to excess. And in sensitive individuals it may cause a condition sometimes known as "tobacco heart," characterized by palpitations and irregularities in beat. None of these conditions are particularly serious, but they may be uncomfortable. The association of cigarette smoking and lung cancer appears established in rather convincing-looking statistics, but eminent statisticians still question their validity.

During the early weeks of pregnancy, when a woman is suffering from nausea, the smell or taste of cigarettes is apt to be offensive. Women frequently voluntarily give up smoking at this time (and sometimes force their husbands to do likewise).

But if you find smoking a pleasure, and do not regard the inconveniences and annoyances it may bring as of any great consequence, you can continue to enjoy smoking with a clear conscience as far as the health of your baby is concerned.

Liquor. Moderate indulgence in alcohol has no harmful effect either upon the mother or the unborn child. Alcohol in quantities insufficient to cause intoxication is consumed rapidly by the body as a food. The small amount that gets into the circulation of the unborn child is rapidly eliminated.

You should not be afraid that indulgence in the cocktail before dinner or other moderate drinking is likely to cause any alcoholic tendency in your child. Alcoholism is merely one form of neurosis, which may tend to run in families but has no connection with the drinking of alcohol by the mother-to-be.

Drinking to the point of intoxication, however, is most unwise during pregnancy. No cases have been reported in which drunkenness alone caused any serious harm to mother or unborn child. But intoxication makes a person more prone to accidental injury. And a severe hangover, especially during the early months of pregnancy, is apt to be more distressing than at any other time.

Medication. Every pregnant woman is concerned lest medication prescribed for her do harm to her unborn child. This anxiety is nothing new. But it has been increased a thousandfold since the tragedy of Thalidomide. Here was a tranquilizing drug considered so safe that it was sold in Europe without prescription. And its danger to the developing embryo was not recognized until some ten thousand babies had been horribly deformed.

As a natural result of this tragedy, confidence in all drugs has been shaken, and even commonly used medications have been brought under suspicion on the flimsiest of evidence.

No mother-to-be wishes to expose her child to the slightest danger in order to spare herself some minor discomfort. And probably no harm will be done if a tendency to over-medication is curbed. However, in order to retain our sense of proportion it should be pointed out that the effect of Thalidomide—a drug never released in this country—is apparently unique. During the past thirty years when so many new medications were introduced, perinatal mortality (which includes the loss of babies before labor, at birth and in the first month of life) has been greatly *reduced* in this country. And the number of babies born with congenital defects has *not* increased.

This could hardly be the case if drugs such as Bonamine, prescribed in hundreds of millions of doses, had been causing significant damage. When you read newspaper headlines that cast suspicion on well-known medications, remember that fear often sells newspapers. At the present time there is *no* evidence that any medication ever legally prescribed in this country has done harm to the developing embryo. The only exceptions to this are certain dangerous anti-

leukemia medications given deliberately to produce therapeutic abortion.

The commonly used medications—laxatives, aspirin, anti-
histamines, sleeping pills and tranquilizers—may be continued in pregnancy in the usual doses. No medication likely
to be prescribed by your obstetrician can harm the unborn
child.

DIET

What is a proper pregnancy diet? Probably at no other
time in adult life is so much attention paid to diet as during
pregnancy. Suddenly every element of food seems to become of vital importance to a woman. She worries about
whether the child inside her is suffering from malnutrition,
whether she is drinking enough milk to provide a skeleton
for her infant, whether she herself needs more of some
food element because her baby is robbing her of it. I would
venture to guess that at least 75 per cent of all pregnant
women take—in addition to their normal foods—some form
of capsule which is guaranteed to assure the minimum re-
quirements of all vitamins, calcium, phosphorus, iron and
other less well-known minerals.

My own feeling is that the young woman whose diet
has been adequate up to pregnancy—as indicated by good
physical development, proper height-weight ratio, etc.—is not
likely suddenly to go seriously wrong in her diet simply
because she has become pregnant.

It is true that in the first three months of pregnancy,
when you are suffering from nausea, your diet may be relatively poor. You may even lose a few pounds. Under these
circumstances, your obstetrician may add a vitamin supplement to your diet. If the taste of the vitamins is offensive
to you, they can be given by injection.

Similarly, if you have some special weight or health problem, your doctor will advise you about a special diet—
whether it involves eliminating certain foods from your
diet, or taking certain minerals or vitamins—which will help
you.

But for the average woman, a proper diet during pregnancy
is no different from a proper diet when she is not pregnant.
Your diet should include a good portion of meat, fish, or

eggs every day. Sufficient bulk from leafy vegetables serves as an aid to natural elimination; it helps avoid dependence on laxatives. Grain products, such as breadstuffs and cereals, though popularly frowned upon as starch, actually contain considerable protein and are useful foods. It is not for nothing that bread was called the staff of life.

Radically altering your customary diet because you are pregnant is likely to bring on digestive disturbances. The intestinal tract is accustomed to a certain amount of bulk, roughage, and fluid. A very much altered diet can cause unnecessary discomfort in the form of diarrhea, constipation, and gas pains.

Milk. Milk is a good food if you enjoy it. If you are not inclined to obesity, there is no objection to your drinking as much as you like. If you are overweight, you may substitute skimmed milk. If you detest milk in all its forms and it does not appear to agree with you, there is no reason why you should be forced to consume it. There are other calcium-containing foods, such as the milk products that are used in cooking, ice cream, and the usual pregnancy combination of vitamins and minerals.

The importance of calcium in the diet of the pregnant woman has usually been overstressed. If a woman is not taking her calcium in capsule or tablet form, she is urged to consume at least one quart of milk a day. The impression conveyed is that the infant to be born is to be constructed of solid limestone. The truth is that the fetus contains a very modest amount of calcium up to the final months of pregnancy. It is only then that the bone structure begins to lay down relatively large quantities of calcium. Recent work has indicated that, because of milk's high phosphorus content, there may actually be less calcium absorbed in the system when large quantities of milk are consumed than when milk drinking is more moderate.

Water and salt. It has been suggested that pregnant women should drink unusually large quantities of water in order to keep the urinary tract well flushed. Under normal conditions, your own natural inclinations are a perfectly good guide and need not be exceeded. If you have a tendency to constipation, however, increased consumption of water may help.

Your salt intake should not be restricted in excessively hot weather, when you perspire a great deal. At such times you need your salt. But the influence of pregnancy on your hormones causes you to retain salt. If you eat excessive amounts of salt or salty foods, you may develop swelling (especially of the ankles) resulting from accumulation of body fluid. This is called edema. It happens when your body has to retain water in order to dilute excess amounts of salt.

Such swellings are not necessarily of any serious significance—unless accompanied by other symptoms: headaches, albumen in the urine, and elevation of blood pressure. But it is uncomfortable and unsightly. If your ankles do become swollen, you should eliminate salt from your diet as much as possible.

Though the swelling is caused by retention of fluid, you do not have to curtail the amount of liquid you drink. Your body can always excrete excess water. It only retains water when it has to, in order to dilute the salt you have retained.

Your weight during pregnancy. The American diet is unusually high in proteins and calories. Under normal circumstances it is certainly adequate for pregnancy.

Special diets that are prescribed for pregnancy can lead to overeating if a woman takes them too literally. Such diets insist that the pregnant woman must drink a quart of milk a day and take generous portions of meat, cereal, and other nourishing foods—in amounts that bring her caloric intake up to the maximum. If she ate only what the diet prescribed, she would do very well. But most women, even though eating the full amount prescribed by the diet, will also indulge to some extent their perfectly natural desire for sweets and desserts. The result will be a caloric intake that is far too high for good health.

The appetite of a normal woman is a fairly good guide to her diet. If you have an ice-cream soda, and consequently have less appetite for dinner, do not feel that you must force down every item mentioned by pregnancy diets to get the proper amount of nourishment from that dinner. That would be overeating. You already received *some* of your required nourishment from that soda.

Under normal circumstances a woman can gain between twenty and twenty-five pounds during the course of pregnancy. Part of this weight is accounted for by the weight of the baby. The rest is accounted for by the placenta, the bag of waters, the enlargement of the uterus, increased fluid in the body tissues, and a small amount of extra fat deposit.

Almost all this weight will be lost automatically within a week or two following delivery of the baby.

But if you increase the amount of food you normally eat to take in everything prescribed in pregnancy diets, and still continue to indulge as usual in sweets, liquor, and snacks, your caloric intake may rise to 1,000 or 1,500 calories a day more than you should be taking. The chances are then that you will gain much more than twenty to twenty-five pounds during your pregnancy. The extra weight will be fat. Obesity is frowned upon by all medical authorities—and insurance companies—as increasing the risk of all diseases. This holds true in pregnancy. Toxemia of pregnancy is more common among overweight women.

Furthermore, no young woman would be happy if she found, after her pregnancy was over, that she had lost her youthful figure and gained unsightly fat. This is not a necessary part of having a baby.

If you are overweight. The problem of diet for the woman who is already considerably overweight when she undertakes pregnancy should be discussed with her obstetrician. If you are overweight, there is no reason why you should not go on a reduced-calorie diet during your pregnancy.

You must, of course, continue to take adequate amounts of proteins, the building materials for your child. (High-protein foods include milk, cheese, eggs, meat, fish, poultry.) You must also eat sufficient amounts of carbohydrates (sugar, starches) so that excessive combustion of your own fat will not tend to produce an acidosis. But you can, with a well-balanced diet, get enough protein and carbohydrates, and at the same time keep your caloric intake low. You can actually lose weight during pregnancy and still have a perfectly well-formed and healthy child.

But since you will be greatly restricting your bulk and caloric intake on such a diet you must be sure to take a vitamin and mineral supplement to insure against deficiency.

In controlling the weight of an overweight woman during pregnancy, it is perfectly safe to take the usually prescribed appetite-curbing drugs. These have not been shown to have any harmful effect whatsoever on mother or child.

At the very least, if an overweight woman manages to avoid *gaining* any weight in pregnancy, she will find after

giving birth that she has actually *lost* about twenty pounds—
and is that much improved.

If you are underweight. Underweight women should try
to gain as much weight as possible during pregnancy. If you
are ten or twenty pounds underweight, and you gain forty
pounds during pregnancy, you may retain fifteen or twenty
of these extra pounds after the pregnancy is over. You will
enjoy better health and appearance as a result.

Some women are afraid that if they gain too much weight,
their baby will be larger, making delivery harder. There is no
significant relationship between weight gained in pregnancy
and the size of your child. There is no reason to believe that
if you gain forty pounds you will have a larger baby than if
you gained only twenty pounds. Even if the increased
amounts of food you ate during pregnancy could make your
baby somewhat fatter, this would not have much effect on
the difficulty of delivery. The largest portion of the baby is
the head, on which there is not—certainly not in infancy—
any deposit of fat.

So if you are underweight, discuss a weight-gaining diet
with your obstetrician. Even if you have been unable to gain
weight before, you may find that you can gain weight while
pregnant—and keep some of it after your baby is born.

One final word on diets in general. Whether you are underweight, overweight, or just feel you should be observing a different diet because of your pregnancy—do not undertake any
special type of diet until you have consulted your doctor
about it. If he agrees that a change in your diet is called for
during your pregnancy, he will prescribe the changes in diet
that are required—and safe—in *your* particular case.

CHAPTER 9

Common Discomforts and Difficulties

Nausea. Some claim that the nausea of pregnancy is psychological: A little girl may be told that babies grow in the stomach. When she grows up and becomes pregnant, if she is afraid and wishes to reject the child, she subconsciously thinks that she can get the child out of her stomach by vomiting.

This is a very scientific way of saying it is all in your head. In my experience, this is far from the truth. Nausea of pregnancy is just as real as motion sickness or mountain sickness, or any of the other symptoms that some people must undergo when their bodies are adapting to changing conditions.

It is true that symptoms may vary in great degree and that there are people who can go through fairly violent changes without any. But this does not prove that those who do suffer are suffering for psychological reasons. Many a child who saw playmates having fun on a merry-go-round had not the faintest inkling that the motion would make him ill until he tried it. Those travelers who become ill when visiting such high places as Mexico City have no visual indication of the altitude that is reducing their oxygen.

However, nausea is very easily conditioned. It rapidly becomes associated with the surroundings under which it occurred. A person who never had seasickness might be perfectly at ease aboard a ship until its movement made him ill. But if he became sick enough on that voyage, the next time he stepped aboard a ship, even while it was tied to the dock and motionless, certain characteristic odors could quickly recall the sensations of the previous trip and bring on nausea.

The same thing may easily occur in pregnancy. Women become nauseated because of the internal changes going on within their bodies. During the period of nausea, any strong odors—food, cigarettes, coffee, bacon—may accentuate the feeling just as they will with nausea of any origin (such as infection of the liver). Eventually, the body of a pregnant woman adapts itself to the changes, and the physical basis for her nausea disappears. The same thing happens in mountain sickness: The body eventually makes its adaptation to the lower oxygen pressure at high altitudes.

However, during the early sensitive phase, the nausea often becomes associated with certain odors, foods, surroundings, people, or even such simple occupations as brushing the teeth. This association may become so strongly bound that after the physical basis of nausea has vanished, the feeling of nausea returns as a conditioned reflex. A person who has once been seasick can get sick again just by looking at a stationary painting of a ship upon a rough sea.

It is not possible to say at what point in any particular pregnancy the nausea ceases to be physiological and becomes psychological. In most pregnancies, the worst nausea is over by the end of two and a half to three months. But minor manifestations—such as a bad taste in the mouth, increased secretions of mucus with a tendency to gag on rising in the morning—may continue throughout pregnancy.

"Morning sickness" is the term so often applied to the nausea of pregnancy, although in some cases it grows worse during the day. Not infrequently it is aggravated by fatigue, so that the woman suffers most in the evening. No matter how severe the nausea may be you should not be afraid that vomiting will cause you to miscarry. A normal growing embryo—as I have said before in this book—is a stubborn survivor. Vomiting will not harm your baby so long as adequate nutrition is maintained.

There are rare extreme cases of vomiting of pregnancy that require hospital treatment. In such cases there is almost always a strong psychological factor as well as the physical basis. But this makes the condition nonetheless dangerous. Before the days when vitamins were available in an injectible form, long-continued vomiting, with inability to take anywhere near adequate amounts of vitamins, proteins, and calories, could lead to a state that might even prove fatal. When the doctor felt that such a condition was approaching, it was sometimes necessary to perform an abortion to save the mother's life.

Under modern conditions, such an outcome is practically unheard of. It is possible in today's hospitals to feed women intravenously. This will not give them sufficient calories to maintain their weight, but it does give them enough fluids, salts, glucose, and vitamins so that, supplemented by a minimum amount of food intake by mouth, they can be tided over this dangerous period. When it has passed, an adequate diet can again be taken by mouth.

Although very few will require such treatment, almost every pregnant woman experiences some degree of nausea. There are a number of ways in which it can be minimized.

If your nausea is particularly severe when you wake up in the morning, eat something before you get out of bed. It should be something dry, bland, and a little filling. You can leave some saltines or pieces of melba toast beside your bed before you retire at night. If your husband can bring you some oatmeal to eat in bed, that may help. Don't take anything sharp, such as fruit juices.

After you have eaten something on awakening, stay in bed for at least another half-hour. Don't get up right away with that empty feeling in your stomach. A sensation of hunger is soon transformed into definite nausea.

During the day, too, it is important never to allow your stomach to feel empty. Keep some cookies handy, something to nibble on wherever you are. Try to take small, frequent feedings instead of sitting down to one big, complete meal. And when you do have nausea, stay away from liquids.

Fatigue will also aggravate nausea and make you more susceptible to it. So it is wise for you to go to bed early. And take a rest period during the day if at all possible.

Drugs are available that are frequently effective, although there is no one medication that works for every woman.

For evening nausea, the motion sickness drugs like Dramamine and Bonamine can be helpful, as well as certain of the tranquilizers related to thorazine. Since they also cause some drowsiness, these drugs have an added advantage for evening use: they may help you to get a good night's sleep.

But because of this drowsiness-producing quality they are not so desirable during the daytime. If you have to struggle against a feeling of sleepiness during the day, it is apt to make your nausea even more distressing.

For daytime nausea the same drugs that are used to curb the appetite—Dexedrine, Benzedrine, etc.—may be helpful. This is not so strange as it might seem. Hunger and nausea are closely related, both being characterized by contractions of the stomach. It is hard to tell whether the first hollow sensation in the pit of the stomach is a pang of hunger or the onset of nausea. (Don't take *any* drug without your doctor's advice. Most of those mentioned here require a prescription.)

If you suffer from pronounced nausea early in pregnancy, you may find it difficult to maintain a balanced diet. Avoid any and all foods that upset you during the nausea of early pregnancy. If you are a normally healthy woman, and you have observed good nutrition up to the time of pregnancy, your body possesses a large reserve. You will not suffer any severe deficiency in the course of a few weeks, even if your diet is limited to such items as candy, cake, ice cream and snacks. There is almost nothing we eat that does not have value as food.

Nor will such an odd and limited diet during the period of the worst nausea in early pregnancy be likely to harm your baby. In the first two to three months of pregnancy the nutritive demands of the growing fetus are not large.

If you simply cater to your food whims when your stomach feels queasy in early pregnancy, as the nausea passes you will be able to eat everything again and enjoy it. You can then follow a healthful, balanced diet for the remainder of your pregnancy.

But if you try, while you are in this state of nausea, to force down foods that go against the grain, you may develop a fixed aversion to them. This aversion may persist long after the original state of nausea has disappeared. You may then have trouble observing a sensible diet for months to come.

The same thing applies to the taking of vitamins. If you are suffering from nausea in early pregnancy, it is wisest to defer taking vitamins by mouth.

It is probably true that if you are not eating well because you have nausea, you are not receiving enough vitamins. But a previously well-nourished person does not develop a vitamin deficiency overnight.

Practically all vitamin preparations in the form of capsules or pills have a tendency to repeat, with a characteristic flavor that may increase your nausea. This, in turn, will make it even more difficult for you to eat your regular meals. If this happens, your nutrition will be made worse by the use of vitamins, instead of better.

When necessary, vitamin supplements can be given by injection.

Nausea and vomiting in late pregnancy. Characteristically, nausea and vomiting are associated with the first three months of pregnancy. During the middle three months you are apt to enjoy a ravenous appetite and your only problem will be to avoid overeating. But a few women find themselves again somewhat nauseated in the last weeks of pregnancy.

If this symptom is severe, it should immediately be brought to the attention of your obstetrician. In some cases, however, it is simply a reflex, due to the increasing strength of the contractions of the uterus as labor approaches. It is likely to appear in women whose menstrual cramps were associated with nausea and vomiting.

Mouth watering. An uncomfortable symptom that may occur in pregnancy—particularly in nervous women—is excessive salivation. This is frequently related to nausea, but may persist long after the definite sensation of nausea has left. Though not frequent, it is most unpleasant and embarrassing. It may be treated with drugs that decrease the flow of saliva.

Heartburn. Heartburn is by no means an exclusive disability of the pregnant woman. It is something in which her husband can freely share, as a result of overindulgence in food, drink, or worry. It is characterized by a feeling of pressure in the pit of the stomach and a hot, burning feeling rising up under the breastbone to the throat. At times a sour taste accompanies it.

It is not known why this condition is so characteristic of the latter months of pregnancy. One old wives' tale had it that it was a sign that the baby's hair was growing. In practice, however, you see many a bald-headed baby whose mother was a great sufferer from heartburn.

Usually the condition is readily relieved, if only temporarily, by any alkaline medication that neutralizes the excessive acidity of the stomach content. Many of these are available at any drugstore, under the various names of digestive aids. If the condition is severe, your obstetrician will have recourse to more effective medications that require a prescription. Among the simpler remedies that frequently work are a little milk or a half teaspoon of ordinary baking soda.

Constipation. Women troubled with constipation may find that they become more regular when they are pregnant. Other women will have the opposite reaction, and suddenly develop a tendency to constipation.

Constipation is to be avoided, since overdistention of the colon and rectum causes cramps that may stimulate contractions of the uterus. The use of a *mild* laxative is preferable. Laxatives that have too drastic an action can also cause cramps, and should be avoided.

What constitutes a mild laxative is an individual matter. For some women, Cascara may work pleasantly; with others if can cause disagreeable cramps. Two tablespoons of milk of magnesia may always be considered harmless; but in some women it is too weak to be effective. The same applies to use of various trade-marked laxatives that contain phenolphthalein as the active ingredient (their trade names usually begin with Feene...).

The use of mineral oil and mineral-oil emulsions is not harmful in itself unless used too frequently. The danger here lies in the fact that mineral oil has a tendency to dissolve and remove certain essential fat-soluble vitamins, particularly vitamins A and D, before your system can absorb them. If you take mineral oil, minimize this danger by using it only occasionally, and never use it close to mealtime. Also be sure that you are getting adequate amounts of vitamins A and D in your diet at the same time.

You may also use the bulk-forming substances to correct constipation. These are essentially cellulose derivatives. Like paper, they tend to swell, soaking up water and forming a softer and bulkier stool, which improves elimination. When you use any of these artificial bulk producers, be sure to drink large amounts of water to avoid the formation of any hard fecal masses.

Enemas may be taken during pregnancy if it is necessary. But they should be avoided when possible. If you do have to take an enema, use a small amount of water, not more than a pint.

Careful attention to your diet—the adding of more leafy vegetables and fresh fruits—will also help to correct a tendency to constipation.

Strange food cravings. The almost uncontrollable desire for weird or out-of-season foods among pregnant women is encountered far more often in fiction than in practice. I suspect any woman of dramatizing who develops an overwhelming desire for any food that she wasn't normally fond of before she became pregnant.

It is more likely that you may develop strong aversions to foods that were ordinarily acceptable—and thus eat relatively more of other foods. And it is not uncommon during period of nausea to develop cravings for salty, spicy foods, or sweets. Of course the craving for sweets is normally present in many of us anyway, and all we need is an excuse to indulge it.

Stretch marks. During the last months of pregnancy, as your skin draws tight from the pressure of your expanding abdomen, stretch marks may appear in your skin. These are long streaks that may be pink, deep red, or purplish in color. Similar marks may also appear on your breasts, hips, or thighs.

There are on the market various creams to soften the skin, in the hope that this will cause the skin to stretch more evenly without the development of these marks. Firm girdles have also been prescribed. My experience indicates that the cause of these stretch marks is beyond the control of patient or doctor.

Whether such marks appear and the extent to which your skin will be marked depend in part on the amount your abdomen expands because of the size of your baby (or babies), the amount of fluid surrounding your baby, and how much excess fat you acquire. Whether these marks appear on your breasts or not depends on how much bigger and heavier your breasts become. Your hips and thighs may be marked if too much fat collects in these places.

But probably one of the most important factors contributing to the appearance of stretch marks—wherever they develop—is glandular. In certain conditions of overactivity of the adrenal gland, similar marks will appear in women who are not pregnant, and even in men. During pregnancy, the adrenal cortex becomes much more active than at other times, and this certainly contributes to the developing of stretch marks.

The appearance of such stretch marks may be quite distressing to you, since they are deep red or purplish. But after you give birth to your baby, these stretch marks will gradually become smaller, thinner, and lose their red or purple coloring. In time, they will become only faint silvery streaks that are hardly noticeable and not at all disfiguring.

Itching of the skin. At about the same time as stretch marks appear you may be troubled by some amount of irritation or stinging of the skin in the same areas. This is caused by the same thing: the fact that your skin becomes stretched and taut. The creams that are marketed for softening the skin may give you some relief.

Acne. Early in pregnancy acne is likely to recur in women who had it when they were adolescents—though not to the same extent. Some pregnant women suffer from a rash on the face, particularly around the chin. This condition is *temporary*. It usually requires no special treatment, but it should be called to your doctor's attention. He may want to recommend special soaps to minimize the condition.

Red blebs. During the first half of pregnancy some women notice tiny red blood blisters with threadlike red extensions appearing in their skin. These consist of little tufts of dilated capillary blood vessels. They may appear anywhere on the body—on the arms, the trunk, or even on the face. They have no special significance but will tend to persist permanently unless removed with the electric needle of a dermatologist.

"Mask of pregnancy" (*chloasma*). This is a brownish discoloration over the cheekbones, extending up over the bridge of the nose and the forehead. Once established, it persists throughout the remainder of the pregnancy. It fades gradually after birth—like a sunburn fades.

The cause of this condition is not entirely known. It appears to be related to poor nutrition because of its tendency to affect the lower-income groups. When seen among the more well-to-do, it is usually among those who suffer severely from nausea of pregnancy and whose diet, therefore, has tended to be inadequate.

Rashes. During pregnancy there is increased tendency to perspire. The combination of this and the normal weight gain promotes chafing and irritation of the skin between the thighs, under the breasts, under folds of fatty tissues on the abdomen—particularly in hot weather. Treatment is preventive, for the most part: avoidance of excessive weight gain; bathing and powdering those surfaces that are likely to become moist in contact with one another.

. *Moles.* There is often a tendency to develop tiny brownish moles, particularly on the neck and chest. They differ from the familiar moles that tend to be flat. These grow on a stalk so threadlike as to be scarcely visible. They may persist for some time, but are frequently rubbed off with a towel after bathing. A few of the larger ones may have to be removed later on. They have no significance as far as general health is concerned.

Freckles. During pregnancy your skin will take up brown pigment more readily, either from exposure to the sun or wherever there has been any inflammation or scar-tissue formation. A scratched and infected mosquito bite during pregnancy may leave a permanently bronze-colored spot on your skin. Where operations must be undertaken during pregnancy, the scar may remain a permanently dark-brown color.

For this reason, cosmetic operations in exposed areas should not be undertaken during pregnancy. And it is probably best to avoid such procedures as electrolytic removal of hairs, because if an infection should develop it may leave a permanently brown-pigmented scar.

Fatigue. A symptom that is quite normal and generally appears very early in pregnancy is a tendency to tire easily and a need for greater amounts of sleep. You may find yourself nodding very shortly after your evening meal, and may find it difficult to stay awake to your accustomed hour. Don't worry that this is a symptom of anemia, vitamin deficiency, or low blood pressure. It is not. It is a normal symptom of pregnancy, and probably is nature's way of signaling the need for increased rest.

It cannot be cured with vitamins. And it *should not* be treated with continual use of artificial stimulants, which are harmless in themselves but only mask your real need for rest. The *only* proper treatment for this symptom is to obey the impulse and go to bed early.

Insomnia. Early in pregnancy women are likely to complain more of difficulty in staying awake. It is not until the last weeks of pregnancy that sleep is apt to be disturbed. The strong activity of your baby and the pressure of the enlarged abdomen make it difficult for you to find a position in which you can be comfortable for long periods of time. Pressure on the bladder, making it necessary for you to get up several times during the night, may also interfere with getting enough sleep. And of course worry, the chief cause of insomnia at any stage of life, is not necessarily banished during pregnancy.

There is no harm in taking the usual dose of sleeping pills. In fact, trying too hard to do without them sometimes makes insomnia a habit.

Headaches. Headaches during the first three months of pregnancy are likely to occur among women who suffered pre-menstrual headaches. The physiology of pregnancy in its early stages and the pre-menstrual state is quite similar. The exact mechanism involved in either of these two types of headaches is not clear.

Pregnancy is not a preventive for other types of headaches—although usually migraine, like other probably allergic types of discomfort, are less severe during pregnancy.

Persistent headaches should not be ignored during pregnancy, any more than at any other time of life. In the *later* months of pregnancy, if these headaches are accompanied by other symptoms, they may indicate a toxic condition with a rising blood pressure. They should be called to the attention of your obstetrician as soon as possible.

For the *ordinary* headache during pregnancy, such remedies as aspirin are perfectly safe. Any headache pills prescribed for migraine, however, should be checked to be sure they do not contain ergot.

Pressure pains. There is a considerable variety of abdominal discomforts associated with the last weeks of pregnancy, when the baby is growing large and heavy and the abdominal cavity feels crowded. Pain may be felt over the bladder region, where the head of the baby is likely to press. Pains are frequently felt in the hip or the groin. A peculiarly characteristic pain is one that develops along the margin of the lowest rib on either the right or the left side.

None of these types of pain have any particular significance as far as impending labor or organic disease is concerned. They are simply due to changes of posture, relaxation of ligaments, and the expanding mass within the abdomen. The symptoms are not usually too severe, and simple remedies such as aspirin should be sufficient.

Vaginal pains. Sudden stabbing pains in the vagina rarely originate in the uterus. They seldom have anything to do with the pregnancy itself. They are usually referred pains, due to a spasm of the muscles surrounding the rectum and vagina. Such spasms may be initiated by constipation or gas.

Although knifelike pains shooting down the vagina and rectum are not signs that anything is wrong, they may, for a fleeting moment, be of greater intensity than actual labor pains.

Leg cramps. One of the most common discomforts of the last months of pregnancy is to awaken and find the muscles of the calf of the leg tightened into an extremely painful knot. These generally occur in the early hours of the morning, after you have slept for some time, and they are precipitated by conscious or unconscious stretching. They can usually be relieved only by getting out of bed and standing with the sole of your foot flat upon the floor.

For want of a better explanation, some medical men have attributed the prevalence of these cramps to calcium deficiency. In newborn infants, or in individuals suffering from lack of parathyroid-gland function, a low level of calcium in the blood will bring on a condition known as tetany. This is characterized by excessive irritability of muscles. Persons suffering from tetany may have a seizure brought on by overbreathing (such as the effort involved in blowing up balloons, which makes even a normal person dizzy). This, by blowing out carbon dioxide and reducing its concentration in the blood, will further lower the concentration of calcium. Such a person goes into a typical spasm of tetany—which consists of a cramping of *both* the arms and the legs.

The muscle cramps of pregnant women, however, are always confined to the lower extremities—the calf of the leg or the foot. There is a change in the circulation of the lower extremities during pregnancy, since the veins that return the blood from the legs drain into the same system of veins that carry the enormously increased volume of blood from the uterus. These cramps occur at night because the circulation in your legs depends to a great extent on muscular *activity*. The contractions of the muscles squeeze the blood forward in the veins, since the backflow is prevented by a system of valves. At night, with your legs at rest, the circulation becomes more sluggish. It is further slowed by the tendency of the pregnant woman to lie on her back, with her increased weight causing more pressure on veins. After some hours of lying relatively immobile, the muscles become quite irritable. Any unwary stretching may lead to a painful cramp.

It is difficult to ascertain whether—as has been claimed— these cramps are controlled by increasing the amount of available calcium. Their frequency tends to diminish as pregnancy continues—with or without a change in calcium intake. I suspect that because of the painful association of stretching with cramps, women soon learn to withstand the urge to stretch their legs, even when semiconscious with sleep.

Back pains. One type of pain that is common in pregnancy is a sciatic pain—a dull ache radiating down one of the buttocks into the thigh. This usually appears in about the fourth month of pregnancy. It does not last for more than a few weeks. It usually disturbs a woman very little once she is assured that it has no dire importance.

This pain is possibly due to the relaxation of the ligaments that bind the bones of the pelvic girdle together. One of the hormones secreted early in pregnancy—known as "relaxin"—has this effect. The function of this relaxation of the ligaments is to make the pelvis potentially roomier. It relaxes the bonds between the bones that make up this ring through which the baby must pass at birth. In doing so, it probably allows some unaccustomed play to the sacroiliac hinges, causing some degree of nerve pinching and sciatic pain.

The only treatment is application of gentle heat, aspirin, and reassurance.

Backache. Most women complain of backache at one time or another during their lives. It can be brought on by a variety of causes. Nature certainly never designed one sex to walk upon heels artificially elevated to a height of two or three inches. This may be an important predisposing cause of backache. The wearing of high heels causes exaggerated arching of the back in order to keep the body in balance. During pregnancy, with the weight of your growing baby extending out in front, your back has to be still further arched. This can lead to backache.

One answer is to try to get used to lower heels. But this is not always a practical solution. From many years of wearing high heels, the Achilles tendons become somewhat shortened. Suddenly changing to low heels will cause a pull along the muscles at the back of the thighs and the calves of the legs—and further discomfort.

Poor posture in general is responsible for backache at any time of life. Such backache is increased when carrying burdens—either outside or inside the body.

Women's back muscles have become accustomed to the

support of a girdle, which helps to improve posture. Early in pregnancy the regular girdle may become uncomfortable. You may feel hesitant about getting into a maternity girdle, particularly in the summer. But attempting to do without a girdle, when you are used to one, can increase back discomfort.

Vaginal secretions and irritation. It is normal during pregnancy for the amount of vaginal secretion to be increased. It may sometimes give you an uncomfortable moist feeling. But this is nothing to worry about, and there is nothing to be done about it.

Pregnant women also frequently complain that their vagina has a strong odor (usually urinous). In most cases this appears to be no more than an exaggerated sensitivity to smells that accompanies the nausea of early pregnancy.

In addition to this normal increase in vaginal discharge and hypersensitivity to normal odors there is a tendency during pregnancy for certain vaginal infections to develop. When such a condition does occur, you will experience distressing itching about the vagina. You cannot treat this condition yourself. You absolutely must not use a douche of your own accord. Call your obstetrician, and go to him for treatment.

One type of vaginal infection that is responsible for an itching yellow discharge during pregnancy is due to a yeast or mold (monilia) with the scientific name of *candida albicans.* This infection does not come about through contact with any particular infected material, for this mold exists everywhere. It infects the vagina because the chemical conditions during pregnancy are favorable to its growth, just as an open vat of grapejuice will attract the type of bacteria that will cause it to ferment.

The growth of this mold may be accelerated by the use of antibiotics for treatment of other conditions. These kill off competing organisms but do not affect this yeast form. Therefore, its growth is unimpeded. This infection exists to some degree in the vaginas of a large percentage of pregnant women—even without symptoms. It is probably the source of a mild infection of the mouths of newborn babies, known as thrush. Thrush is not serious and responds quickly to treatment by the pediatrician or family doctor.

The mold infection of the vagina is readily relieved by treatment. But in some cases it may prove stubborn and show a tendency to recur from time to time.

White vaginal discharge. The discharge associated with infection is usually yellow, because pus, which is exuded from an infected wound or an infected surface, is ordinarily yellow to yellowish green in color. An excessive amount of *white* discharge from the vagina, on the other hand, is normally not due to an infection, but to an oversecretion of mucus—usually under nervous stimulation.

Mucus is normally water clear, but in the vagina it becomes mixed with the castoff white cells that form the lining of the vagina, and assumes a milky appearance. The casting off of these cells from the vaginal lining is a perfectly normal process, just as the casting off of the horny surface layer of cells from the skin that is noted after taking a bath.

Frequency of urination. Quite early in pregnancy, shortly after missing a period, women characteristically notice that they have to urinate more often. At this stage it is probably the result of changes in body chemistry that are taking place.

During the middle months of pregnancy it is not particularly noticeable. However, in the last three months, when the baby exerts significant pressure on the bladder as soon as it contains any quantity of urine, frequency of urination may become more annoying. You may have to get up once or twice during the night. You may notice, particularly in subsequent pregnancies, a tendency to lose control of urine if you cough, laugh, or sneeze when the bladder is full.

Varicose veins. Probably the most important preventive against the development of varicose veins during pregnancy is selection of proper ancestors. There is no question but that the tendency to develop varicose veins is hereditary.

Varicose veins should not be confused with the more prominent veins that every pregnant woman will note, which are due simply to the increased volume of blood. True varicose veins become raised above the surface, causing a discoloration of the overlying skin and various types of discomforts: itching near the veins, actual pain over the veins, or a dull, tired feeling in the leg involved.

There is no way in which a woman unfortunate enough to have an inherited tendency can prevent the development of varicose veins. Round garters, which constrict the veins and act as a tourniquet, may, however, produce varicose veins even if you do not have such a tendency.

Elastic stockings may make the person suffering from varicose veins much more comfortable. However, they cannot be used to *prevent* their development. Nor will they cure the veins already varicose. At best, they are a device for minimizing the discomfort until more definite surgical treatment can be given.

In some cases it is considered advisable to treat varicose veins even during pregnancy—by injections or other forms of surgical treatment. In most instances, where the discomfort is not too severe, it is wisest to wait and see how much improvement takes place spontaneously when the pregnancy is over. Once definite varicose veins have developed they are not likely to disappear completely. However, they do become much less prominent and cause much less discomfort.

Superficial dilated vessels, appearing on the thighs or about the ankles as tiny groups of wavy purplish threads, are of no significance. They are not to be considered as varicose veins, and are distressing only from the cosmetic standpoint. It may be comforting to know that they will be well hidden by a good sun tan if that part of the anatomy is necessarily exposed.

Hemorrhoids (*piles*). These represent nothing more than additional branches of the system of veins—in this case surrounding the anus. They drain into the distended pelvic veins and become subject to greater back pressure during pregnancy.

Hereditary factors play a part, but pregnancy will accelerate the tendency to develop hemorrhoids. It is doubtful whether good bowel habits can absolutely prevent their development, but constipation or diarrhea can aggravate the symptoms.

Ordinarily, hemorrhoids cause a dull, nagging pain or a feeling of pressure about the anus. They tend to protrude on straining, and may remain swollen and tender.

If a sudden pain that is particularly severe and persistent develops, it usually means that a clot has formed in one of these veins. Ointments and suppositories will give little relief. The best treatment is to soak in warm baths to relax the spasm of the muscles surrounding the anus. To avoid aggravating the condition further, curtail your activities until the acute symptoms subside in three or four days.

Slight bleeding from the rectum is usually interpreted as meaning hemorrhoids. But actually the hemorrhoids themselves rarely bleed. Bleeding is due to a cracking of the skin of the anus, usually associated with constipation and spasm of the muscle surrounding the anus. It may occur with or without hemorrhoids. This condition is usually relieved by proper attention to diet to relieve constipation, and by the use of some bland ointment or soothing suppository.

Shortness of breath. This symptom frequently appears rather early in pregnancy. It is probably due to the rapid increase in the volume of circulating blood, which is characteristic of the changed metabolism of pregnancy.

A pregnant woman feels as if she has just finished a heavy meal. She is inclined to breathe more heavily on exertion. As the body adapts itself to the increased blood volume during the middle months of pregnancy, this symptom is likely to become less prominent. But towards the end of pregnancy there is a large weight to be carried, and there is upward pressure against the diaphragm from the baby who is now approaching its full size. Both of these conditions make for shortness of breath—exertion with the increased load, and pressure against the diaphragm when attempting to lie down and rest.

Swelling of the ankles. Owing to the increase in body fluids during pregnancy, most women will be aware of some degree of swelling of the ankles—especially toward the end of a day. This is apparent to an even greater extent during hot weather.

Usually, this is of no serious significance. It is a relatively normal occurrence, which in itself does not imply any toxic condition. It may be reduced in degree by restricting the amount of salt in your diet. If this is not sufficiently effective your physician may prescribe a *diuretic* pill to increase excretion of water and salt.

It *may,* however, accompany toxemia, so it should always be reported to your obstetrician when it first occurs. When accompanied by a feeling of illness, or marked swelling of hands and face, blurring of vision, or reduced output of urine, it is always a sign of a toxic condition and should be reported to your doctor *at once*.

Dizzy Spells. During pregnancy the network of vessels carrying blood is greatly expanded. The body becomes less able to make rapid adjustments to changed conditions. As a result, there may be a relative lack of blood supply to the brain for a moment, causing a blacking-out, which can range from a feeling of dizziness to a complete faint.

To understand this, think in terms of aviation medicine—

and the flier's "G-suit." The flier, whose body is subjected to strong force due to a rapid turn of a fast-moving plane, or in pulling out of a dive, must wear a special suit. It keeps his blood from being forced out of the vessels of his brain and pooling in his abdominal cavity and legs to cause a black-out.

Nature provides humans with an internal "G-suit" that can cope with less-violent forces. If you are in a squatting position, less blood can be contained in your abdominal cavity. Other vessels in the body—including those in the brain—dilate to accommodate more blood supply. When you stand up suddenly, the capacity of your abdominal cavity is greatly increased. Blood flows into it from the other vessels of the body, and your brain becomes relatively anemic for a moment. You may feel dizzy or see bright dots swarming in front of your eyes—symptoms of cerebral anemia. But your body makes such a rapid compensation, constricting the vessels and forcing the blood back up into the brain, that these symptoms are only momentary.

With the greatly increased pool of blood that must be kept available for your growing baby and pregnant uterus, however, your body cannot make these changes quite so rapidly. Dizzy spells and faintness become much more common as a result.

The treatment for a lack of blood to the brain is to assume a position in which the blood reaches the brain more easily. If you feel faint or dizzy, lie down with your head lower than the rest of your body. Usually, the condition corrects itself quickly.

What has been said so far applies to the *brief* spell of dizziness or faintness brought on by long standing, hunger, crowds, heat, and so forth—spells that quickly pass off when the circumstances are changed. Any *persistent* dizziness or prolonged feeling of faintness which is not easily corrected by such simple measures as lying down, cold compresses, aromatic spirits, a drink, should be reported to your doctor immediately.

Body heat. The average woman tends to be more "cold-blooded" than her husband. It is true that she goes about with considerably less clothing, and seems able to tolerate outdoor cold with whatever protection fashion dictates. But in her home she is the one who first wants the windows closed, the heat turned up a little, the extra blanket on the bed, and a warm spot for her icy feet during the night.

During the first few months of pregnancy this changes very little. In fact, these tendencies may be increased. But in the last half of pregnancy a remarkable change takes place. Suddenly this very same woman becomes a fresh-air fiend. The room is always too warm for her. Windows must be opened, covers are thrown off, and for the first time in her life her hands and feet are constantly warm.

Exactly what the nature of this fundamental change may be is a matter of speculation. The basal metabolic rate is increased, and the young growing organism within you generates considerable heat. Your blood volume is greatly increased, and there is probably a greater concentration near the surface. The net effect of these changes does make the pregnant woman feel much warmer and perspire more easily —particularly in the seventh, eighth, and ninth months.

Such a change has nothing to do with any change in your blood pressure—either rise or fall.

Chills and fever. A chill, with a rise in temperature, is always a sign of infection. There *is* such a thing as a nervous shaking chill, not associated with fever, which has no significance whether you are pregnant or not. But a chill followed by a rise in temperature calls for a general examination to discover the source of infection. During pregnancy an infection of the kidney known as pyelitis is the most common cause, but whether it is this or something else that is the cause in any particular case can only be determined by examination.

Nose stuffiness. Frequently women complain of an annoying stuffiness of the nose in early pregnancy. This must be treated the same as you would treat the nasal congestion of a cold or an allergic condition—using nose drops that allow you to breathe comfortably. Any nose drop that shrinks mucous membrane can be abused. If used too often, it will lose its effect and act as an irritant. Where possible, it should be reserved for use on going to bed at night, because at that time the open airway is most essential to comfort.

This condition may persist for three or four months. If it is not associated with any other special condition or allergy, it will tend to improve during the second half of pregnancy.

CHAPTER 10

Illness in Pregnancy

Common infections. Pregnancy confers no immunity against common infections. Colds are just as frequent among pregnant women as among the non-pregnant, and there is no reason why the treatment should not be exactly the same. The usual nose drops, cough syrups, anti-histamines, aspirin or related compounds may be used without harmful effect on the pregnancy.

Antibiotics, however, should be used with caution for minor infections. And they should not be used when it seems likely that recovery will be uncomplicated without them. For use of antibiotics during pregnancy carries with it the danger of causing distressing vaginal itching. By killing off many of the harmlessly competing organisms in the vagina they encourage the overgrowth of a resistant yeast form, Monilia.

In any *serious* infection, which calls for the use of antibiotics, they must be used in spite of the possibility of this annoyance. Such diseases as typhoid fever and lobar pneumonia—with high fever and toxic effects—carry with them the danger of miscarriage or premature labor.

But most of the common infections—such as the intestinal virus diseases that cause vomiting and diarrhea, mild cases of influenza, "grippe," temperatures associated with mild upper respiratory infections—will have no harmful effect upon the growth of the baby.

German measles. German measles is the only disease that has been definitely implicated in causing malformations of the developing embryo. The greatest danger is in the first three months of pregnancy. After three months have gone by there is a good chance that the baby will not be affected.

In the first three months of pregnancy—if we are to believe the statistics, most of which came from Australia during the war years—there is as high as an 85-per-cent incidence of defects in the developing fetus. These range from cataracts in the eyes to malformations of the heart and misshaping of the head. Since German measles has been such a well-known disease for so many years, it is a little hard to explain why it took so long to recognize its effect on the fetus. Some medical men have theorized that the virus changed its character in recent years, and acquired this new virulence.

Ever since these original figures were published, the tendency of many doctors has been to take no chances, to interrupt the pregnancy when the mother suffered definite German measles in the first three months. Once this has been done, there is no way of determining whether a congenital defect would have occurred, since the fetus is destroyed in the interruption of the pregnancy. The law has never actually sanctioned such interruption of pregnancy. But—justifiably or not—many physicians have had no ethical scruples against destroying the life of what they were convinced would develop into a defective individual.

At the present time there is again a doubt as to whether the danger is as grave as it has been depicted. The health department of the City of New York has been very closely following cases of German measles acquired in the first three months of pregnancy—where the pregnancy was allowed to continue. In the thirteen cases followed so far there have been no defects in the infants. Whether there was some mistake in the original calculations of the risk, whether the statistics were in some way distorted by the type of inquiry used, I do not know. But there is more and more evidence that—in this country at least—German measles in the first three months of pregnancy does not involve as high a risk of fetal abnormality as was previously thought.

Every effort should certainly be made to avoid the risk of acquiring German measles during pregnancy. Young girls and non-pregnant women should be deliberately exposed to German measles so that they may be infected and acquire an immunity. If a pregnant woman who has not acquired immunity is exposed to German measles, she is given immune globulin. This is a fraction of the blood obtained from pooled blood of many humans, most of whom naturally would have had German measles at some time during their lives. This type of globulin has a protective action against German measles if given in sufficient quantities and soon enough after exposure.

Operations during pregnancy. If a condition requiring surgery arises during pregnancy, you may have an operation with as much safety as when you are not pregnant. Even abdominal operations will not harm the development of the baby inside you.

An acutely inflamed appendix must be removed, and this may be done with complete safety. Before the days of sulfa and antibiotics it was one of the most feared complications of pregnancy. If it ruptured, this would frequently set up uterine contractions and precipitate labor, which seemed to spread the infection, causing general peritonitis and a fatal outcome. But today, with prompt control of the infection with sulfa or antibiotics, an appendectomy rarely involves any complications as far as the pregnancy is concerned.

Cysts of the ovary are sometimes discovered at the first visit to the obstetrician. If the cyst is no more than two or three inches in diameter, he may simply keep checking on it at subsequent visits. In some cases, the cyst will disappear as the pregnancy develops. But *large* cysts are best removed (by abdominal operation) before an emergency develops. Such cysts do not disappear spontaneously. Delay only increases the possibility of severe pain arising from twisting of the cyst, which cuts off its blood supply. If cysts grow large enough they may even obstruct labor, or rupture during labor, causing peritonitis.

It is usually advisable to wait until the fourth month of pregnancy before removing such cysts. For the cyst may be in the ovary from which the fertilized egg was originally extruded. This ovary contains the gland known as the corpus luteum, which is the remains of the egg follicle. During the first three months it is important for the maintenance of the pregnancy. After three months the placenta takes over production of the hormones that formerly were produced by this ovary. At this time, even if removal of the cyst requires removal of the ovary containing the corpus luteum, the pregnancy will continue without incident.

Intestinal obstruction is very rarely a danger during pregnancy, unless there has been previous abdominal surgery with adhesions between loops of intestine. These may kink as they are displaced by the enlarging uterus. When nausea is accompanied by crampy abdominal pain and distention, do not endure it in silence as part of the discomfort of pregnancy. It should be brought to the attention of your doctor promptly, for it may be caused by intestinal obstruction resulting from such kinking. If the obstruction is complete, an operation is necessary. This is an absolute emergency which must be treated surgically regardless of possible effects on the pregnancy. But with prompt treatment and use of sulfas or antibiotics to control infection, there is no reason why pregnancy should not continue despite such surgery.

Chronic diseases and therapeutic abortion. One of the purposes of having a general physical examination before pregnancy is to discover the presence of any chronic disease that would make pregnancy inadvisable. If chronic disease is not discovered until pregnancy occurs, the question arises as to whether termination of the pregnancy by therapeutic abortion is necessary in the interest of the mother. It is recognized that there are religious objections to the performance of therapeutic abortion under any circumstances. But in all states of this country, whenever the physician believes that continuation of the pregnancy would seriously endanger the life or health of the mother, it is legal for the doctor to perform an abortion.

Heart disease. When heart disease is known to exist, it requires the most careful evaluation to determine whether pregnancy is safe.

A woman need not have too much concern about her ability to have children just because she has had a heart murmur and some evidence of heart disease. Provided she has never been actually incapacitated, and has not been limited in her physical activities, pregnancy should involve no serious risk.

The chief cause of heart trouble among young woman in the childbearing age is rheumatic fever. This may follow a streptococcus infection of the throat. After about a three-week interval joint pains develop that may involve one or more joints. If the heart is affected, one or more of the valves may be deformed, causing leakage or obstruction and interfering with the proper functioning of the heart.

Despite a definite history of rheumatic fever, if a woman

is able to indulge in all forms of exercise (can climb stairs, walk as fast as her friends, dance without shortness of breath) there is every reason to believe that she will be able to go through pregnancy and deliver a child normally. Even though rheumatism has left her with a definite heart murmur, she runs no greater risk than the young woman who has never had heart disease.

Where physical activity *has* had to be limited, where the woman has at some time beeen confined to bed because of failure of the heart to perform its function satisfactorily, where she at times has had to take digitalis or other heart medicine, the risk is carrying through a pregnancy is increased. But the mortality is not high, if she is under careful medical supervision throughout pregnancy.

When the heart is *more* seriously damaged, however—where effort is *always* attended by shortness of breath, where heart medicine has *frequently* had to be taken—the risk of death to the mother in attempting to have a child may be as high as 33 per cent.

The attitude of the medical profession toward pregnancy in women with heart disease has undergone changes in the past ten or fifteen years. At one time it was thought that the ninth month was the most difficult, because the baby was largest at that time. It was believed that the ordeal of labor was the thing most to be feared in pregnancy when the heart had been weakened. But careful studies have shown that the load on the heart increases rapidly around the *fourth* month of pregnancy. As the blood volume expands, the heart has to work harder. Sometimes at this point the woman may have some difficulty and be required to take increased rest. The peak load on the heart is at the end of the *eighth* month. Toward the beginning of the ninth month the volume of blood in the circulation begins to diminish again, and the strain on the heart eases.

It is no longer considered necessary to spare these women the strain of labor by performing Caesarean operations. In fact, it has been found that most women with mild degrees of heart disease go through labor very well. All they need is careful watching to see whether any drugs are needed to aid the heart action during labor, attention to the proper anesthesia, and delivery of the baby as soon as the womb is open to spare the mother the physical labor of bearing down and pushing the baby out as in normal birth.

Again we must stress the point that women with known heart disease require careful observation throughout pregnancy—preferably with obstetrician and heart specialist working as a team. The woman must be impressed with the necessity of adequate rest, a strict diet, and avoiding exposure to infection from any source. A little neglect may seriously burden an already overworked heart.

Today a new method has been found for improving the condition of patients with crippling heart disease due to rheumatic deformities of the heart, known as stenosis. When the affected valve has become narrowed because of the formation of scar tissue, the amount of blood that can pass from one chamber of the heart to the other is greatly reduced. These cases have been dramatically benefited by techniques of modern heart surgery.

The benefits need not be denied to a woman simply because she is pregnant. If the type of heart disease is amenable to surgical treatment, the pregnant woman may undergo heart surgery just as safely as a woman who is not pregnant. The fact that she has undergone this type of surgery will have no bearing on the type of delivery.

It should be added that in some cases women who believe they have heart trouble do not. Many individuals suffer from annoying—or even alarming—discomfort due to episodes of irregular or very rapid heart beat (palpitations). In most such cases, careful examination will reveal no organic heart disease, and pregnancy may be undertaken with perfect safety. Even though the condition persists for years, it does not endanger life.

Kidney disease. Women who have had an episode of acute nephritis following a throat infection or scarlet fever do not necessarily suffer permanent damage to their kidneys. However, women with such a history should have studies done to make sure that the kidney function is adequate for pregnancy. The mere presence of albumen in the urine is not in itself necessarily serious. But any evidence that the kidneys have been severely damaged by a chronic infection—particularly if it is still progressive—absolutely forbids pregnancy.

This condition brings with it anemia and high blood pressure. There may at times be accumulation of nitrogenous wastes due to failure of the kidneys to clear the blood. During pregnancy, the blood pressure is almost certain to rise, the embryo will die in the uterus, and there will be a miscarriage. Further damage is usually done to the kidney of the mother, shortening her life expectancy.

Pus in the urine—known as "pyelitis"—is a common infection in young girls. This usually clears completely without damage to the kidney.

Diabetes. Before the discovery of insulin, young diabetics seldom grew up to marry and bear children. The only diabetics who lived a long time were those in whom the diabetes first appeared during middle age, was not severe, and could be controlled by diet alone.

Today, however, diabetic children are maintained in good health by proper diet and the use of insulin. As a result, diabetic girls do grow up and marry. There are conflicting reports as to how grave the risks are when a diabetic woman undertakes pregnancy. But it is clearly evident that diabetics require the most careful attention throughout, if pregnancy is to have a successful outcome. They must be under the dual care of an obstetrician and an internist or general practitioner.

The dangers to be faced by the diabetic in pregnancy are twofold. First there is the danger that the diabetes itself may become difficult to control. If not carefully watched, the woman may go into acidosis, a condition that is extremely dangerous for the survival of the fetus. The other danger to the diabetic woman is an increased susceptibility to the development of a toxic condition in pregnancy. This is characterized by a sudden rise in blood pressure, headaches, swelling of feet and hands, appearance of albumen in the urine. There is danger to the mother from convulsive seizures. And there is also grave danger to the life of the unborn child.

In addition to this, the diabetic—even under treatment—has a tendency to have children of excessive size. This may make labor difficult and require a Caesarean. Studies have shown that whenever *any* woman has an excessively large baby (ten, eleven, twelve pounds) careful investigation should be undertaken to see if there is a latent diabetes that had been previously unsuspected.

Even when the babies are not excessively large, there is, in the severe diabetic, increased chance of stillbirth. To avoid this, Caesarean section is more frequently resorted to in the final weeks of pregnancy—as soon as the baby seems to be of adequate size.

Tuberculosis. At one time tuberculosis in the mother was one of the most frequent medical indications for terminating a pregnancy. Now it is felt that a tubercular woman can carry through pregnancy without gravely increasing the chance of aggravating the disease. Naturally, if the tuberculosis is at all active, she must be under the strictest medical supervision and absolute bed rest.

If the tuberculosis has been regarded as arrested for some time, then the pregnant woman need observe no more than the usual rules of good hygiene. But her chest should be checked by X ray early in pregnancy, and at any stage when a flare-up is suspected.

No woman with *active* tuberulosis would be advised to become pregnant. Common sense indicates that all except minimal lesions should have been arrested for at least two or three years before pregnancy is contemplated. However, even in the fairly serious case, the present medical opinion is that there is just as great a risk of advancing disease when the pregnancy is terminated as when it is allowed to continue. But it is felt that the stress of *labor* may spread pulmonary disease. Therefore, there is a tendency to resort to a Caesarean for the more advanced types of tuberculosis.

Epilepsy. A woman who knows that she is suffering from epilepsy will be aware of the fact that she has a serious problem—not as regards the pregnancy—but in taking care of the baby. Unless she is perfectly certain that medication can keep her seizures under control, she should defer motherhood or else be certain that someone else can take care of her child until the possibility of seizures is no longer a menace.

Polio. Pregnant women were given a higher priority than other adults when polio vaccine was first produced and the quantity available still limited. The reason for this is that pregnancy seems to lessen the normal immunity of adults against this disease.

There is some question as to whether, when polio strikes a pregnant woman, it is any more severe than the type likely to strike other adults. It does not usually affect the outcome of the pregnancy, except to the extent that it cripples the mother. Mothers have been able to deliver normally even though still in a respirator. In some cases, of course, a Caesarean operation has to be performed under these conditions.

The risk involved depends on how badly crippled the

woman is, on the condition the muscles with which she breathes have been left.

Influenza. Evidence indicates "that influenza may be more serious during pregnancy." It is probably wise to be inoculated with influenza vaccine during the fall months, especially if an epidemic is forecast.

Otosclerosis. This is a form of deafness that usually affects both ears. It is due to a progressive thickening and fusing together of the tiny bones that conduct vibrations from the eardrum to the auditory nerve endings.

The cause of this disease is unknown. The treatment depends on the severity of the hearing defect. Lately there has been considerable success with an operation known as "fenestration." This opens a separate air passage that detours the vibrations around these tiny bones (known as ossicles) directly to the chamber containing the sensitive nerve endings.

Any woman suffering from this form of hearing impairment must realize that her hearing loss is likely to be increased by pregnancy.

Urinary infection. The urinary tract appears to have increased susceptibility to infection during pregnancy. It is not known exactly why this should occur. For a time a mechanical explanation of infection was popular, since the tubes that conduct the urine from the kidneys to the bladder become considerably dilated during pregnancy. It was thought that the heavy weight of the uterus, lying upon these tubes, obstructed the flow of urine and caused the tubes to dilate, and that the stagnating urine became a more suitable medium for bacterial growth.

But actually the uterus does not exert pressure on these tubes. The dilation is apparently due simply to the fact that they are under the same growth stimulation as the uterus in which the baby is developing.

In an effort to overcome this so-called stagnation of urine it has been recommended that the pregnant woman drink very large quantities of water—to keep the urinary tract flushed out so that infection will not develop. There would appear to be very little, if any, scientific support for such a practice. In most instances the sensation of thirst can be regarded as a sufficient guide to the amount of fluid that should be taken. It is doubtful whether forcing undesired quantities of liquid is of any real benefit.

At the present time, under good hygienic conditions,

urinary infection—the so-called "pyelitis" of pregnancy—is not seen with any great frequency. When it does occur, it is in most cases cured rather simply once the suitable antibiotic, sulfa drug, or other chemical is administered. Determination of what organism is causing the infection must be made in order to know which form of medication will eradicate it most effectively.

Effect of pregnancy on blood pressure. Normal pregnancy has little effect on blood pressure. There is a tendency during the early months for the blood pressure to go down a few points, and a tendency for it to rise again in the last months of pregnancy. However, it never goes beyond what are considered the normal limits—unless there is some complicating factor.

Emotions will temporarily affect blood pressure, just as they will affect the pulse rate. Sudden excitement may cause the pulse to race. It may at the same time send the blood pressure high above normal. This is temporary. It comes down with relaxation.

Blood pressure is explained in two figures: the systolic pressure, which is the higher figure, and the diastolic pressure, the lower figure. The pressure in the arteries reaches a peak after the heart has pumped its full content of blood into the circulation; this peak pressure is called systolic pressure, because the contraction of the heart is known as systole. Then, as the valves close and the heart refills with venous blood, the pressure in the arteries drops to a lower level. This is the pressure against which the heart must work to force a new load of blood into the circulation; it is known as the diastolic pressure—the pressure in the arteries when the heart is dilated.

The normal systolic pressure is quite variable. It depends on the age, build, amount of physical activity, nervous condition, and amount of recent rest. Although it was originally stated in some such terms as "a normal of 100 plus your age," this figure has been discarded. Today, for an adult of average build, cardiologists are willing to accept pressures up to 150 as normal systolic pressure—normal in the sense that there is no evidence that it is likely to lead to any disorder of the heart or to shorten the life expectancy.

The diastolic pressure is less subject to fluctuations due to emotion or exercise. The normal range is from 60 to 90.

High blood pressure. There are several causes for high

blood pressure. With severe kidney disease, blood pressure is almost always elevated. In these cases pregnancy is definitely dangerous. There are also rapidly advancing forms of high blood pressure—known as malignant hypertension—which bring on changes in kidneys, blood vessels, eyes, and brain with such rapidity that little space need be devoted to it here; women suffering from this type of high blood pressure would certainly be too ill to become pregnant in the first place.

However, there are large numbers of otherwise healthy women who have a moderately elevated blood pressure. This would mean a pressure—at rest—of more than 140 to 150 systolic, and more than 90 diastolic pressure. Such individuals, male or female, may remain perfectly healthy and without symptoms. If careful investigation reveals no underlying kidney disease there is no great risk involved in pregnancy.

But women beyond their middle thirties who have elevated blood pressure run a greater-than-average risk in pregnancy of developing a condition known as toxemia (see page 152). In this condition the pressure rises still higher and certain changes take place in kidney function. Properly treated, the woman who develops toxemia which is superimposed on high blood pressure runs no grave risk as far as her own life is concerned. But there remains a considerably increased risk of losing her baby.

Low blood pressure. Many women come to an obstetrician stating that they have in the past suffered from low blood pressure and have been given treatments for it. Because they now feel tired, or have some other symptom that may be due to pregnancy, they are under the impression that their blood pressure has again become low. Actually, except as an emergency condition, or in some rare disease of the adrenal gland, there is no such thing as low blood pressure—in the sense of a disabling condition affecting otherwise normal people.

But because the legendary stand of "100 plus your age" has been so popularly accepted, many people are under the impression that if they have a systolic pressure of less than 100 they are suffering from low blood pressure. Such people may have suffered from a variety of ills that brought them to the doctor; the fact that he discovered a blood pressure of under 100 is purely coincidental. Many people are going about enjoying the best of health, completely unaware that their normal blood pressures are at this low figure.

Anemia. The red-colored substance in blood cells that is known as hemoglobin combines with oxygen in the lungs and releases it in the tissues. The measurement of the amount of hemoglobin in the blood determines whether or not a person is anemic.

It has been recognized for many years that the pregnant woman is likely to develop some degree of anemia. One school of thought claims that this is not necessarily a true anemia—that the drop in hemoglobin is due to the fact that the blood, along with the tissues of the body, takes up more water during pregnancy. Its total volume expands, but the blood becomes more dilute. Because of this dilution, an apparent anemia—rather than a real one—develops. There have been many scientific studies with conflicting conclusions about this. Others claim that this anemia is always a true anemia—due to insufficient iron; that it can be prevented by taking sufficient quantities of iron during pregnancy.

No doctor will assume that any anemia is normal. After ruling out more serious types requiring special treatment, he will try a course of iron and vitamins by mouth. For aside from such minor discomforts as constipation—or, less frequently, some degree of diarrhea—such medication can do no harm, even if there is no deficiency. And if there *is* a deficiency, it will help.

The question may be raised of the danger to the baby if the mother *is* anemic, since the infant is dependent upon the materials furnished by the mother's blood stream for its own nourishment and development. Anemia is generally a matter of the hemoglobin content of the mother's red blood cells. These cannot pass across the placental barrier into the circulation of the baby. The only way in which the baby could suffer was if the mother was so anemic that her red cells did not carry enough oxygen.

Toxemia. This is a condition that is peculiar to pregnancy. It has received publicity far out of proportion to the frequency with which it occurs. The fear of toxemia is the reason why so many women are worried when they see swelling of the ankles, or feel the wedding band grow tight as the fingers become somewhat more swollen in the later months of pregnancy.

The cause of toxemia is not completely understood. Endless hours of research have been spent in trying to track it down. The condition usually appears in the last half or third of pregnancy. In the more severe cases it may sometimes appear earlier, particularly in the woman carrying twins.

Toxemia is characterized by a rise in blood pressure. There is accumulation of excessive quantities of fluid in the tissues, causing swelling of the feet, puffiness of the hands and face. It is usually accompanied by headache and a feeling of illness. In the most severe case there are disturbances of vision and a boring type of pain in the pit of the stomach.

Some of these cases, *if untreated,* may go on to what is called eclampsia—sudden convulsions. The term eclampsia comes from the Greek, meaning a bolt of lightning. This description was applied because these convulsions come on so suddenly, with little warning. This condition is extremely dangerous to the life of the mother as well as the unborn child. Fortunately, it is as *uncommon* as swollen ankles are common in pregnancy.

For some reason, which is unknown since the cause of the condition itself remains a mystery, toxemia is largely a disease of the poor. It is seen far more frequently in the wards and clinics than in private practice. Whether this indicates that a poor diet with inadequate vitamin, mineral, or protein intake contributes to it—or whether it is merely a reflection of poor hygienic conditions in general—has not been determined. Poverty is an extremely complex condition, with social, hereditary, and emotional factors not easily analyzed. Among patients one sees in reasonably comfortable circumstances toxemia is rare. But when it does occur it is just as serious. The possibility should never be ignored.

However, many of the *symptoms* that may occur with toxemia are quite common in *normal* pregnancy. You should not become unduly alarmed if you have a simple headache that is promptly relieved by aspirin or similar medication. You should not be alarmed by a little swelling of the ankles appearing in the last two months of pregnancy. Naturally, you should report such conditions to your physician so that he may determine whether there is any other evidence of a toxic condition.

When it has been determined that a real toxemia *exists,* careful treatment is always necessary. Rest—practically complete bed rest—is probably most important, particularly if the condition has appeared while the baby is still too premature to have a good chance for survival. There are a variety of drugs which, when carefully administered, have the effect of reducing high blood pressure, and so lessen the chance of it reaching such peaks that convulsions occur.

If the condition reaches such an extent that the health of the mother is jeopardized, the pregnancy may be terminated in some cases even before the child has a chance of survival. In the very severe cases too much consideration cannot be given to the survival of the infant since the toxemia itself has already lessened the baby's chance to a great degree.

But if the baby has already become sufficiently developed so that its chance of survival is good, the pregnancy would be terminated without hesitation. The baby would be delivered by inducing labor or by performing a Caesarean section.

If the toxemia has not been allowed to continue for too long a time, the symptoms will usually subside promptly after pregnancy. Blood pressure may remain elevated for several weeks, however, before returning to the pre-pregnancy level.

CHAPTER 11

Preparing for Your Baby

TO NURSE OR NOT TO NURSE

Should you breast-feed your baby? Discussion of breast-feeding generates so much emotion that it is difficult to distinguish reason from rationalization. Few mothers of bottle-fed babies appear carefree enough to support the excuse that they "didn't want to be tied down."

At times it seems that the real objection to breast-feeding is a peculiar vestige of old-fashioned prudery. As one woman said, "Why doesn't anyone ever mention the best argument for breast-feeding? *It's fun!*"

Not so very long ago breast feeding was taken for granted. Formulas were poor substitutes. The only form in which milk could be preserved was condensed milk, with its extremely high sugar content. Fresh milk was of uncertain cleanliness and facilities for keeping it were inadequate. If a mother found her own milk supply inadequate, she might have been forced to seek a wet nurse—a woman who had either weaned a child of her own and still had milk in her breasts, or who was able to nurse another infant in addition to her own.

Since that time vast improvements have taken place in the preparation of infant foods. Today, in large cities, probably 90 per cent or more of our babies are raised on artificial formulas. Certainly the woman who does not wish to breast-feed has no reason to feel guilty.

The controversy over nursing has three aspects: The physical effect on the infant, the physical effect on the mother, and the psychological effect on the relationship of mother and child.

As far as the physical effects on the infant are concerned, an obstetrician is not the best-qualified authority. But with so large a percentage of his patients refusing to nurse, he would be bound to hear echoes if bottle feeding caused major difficulties. Certainly, complaints are brought back about feeding problems, but how many of these would have been avoided by breast feeding it is impossible to judge.

Most pediatricians, however, feel that where breast feeding is successful (and there is no way of predicting this for any individual woman) it is probably the ideal method. Some evidence exists that the feeding of foreign protein early in life—in the form of cows' milk—may play a role in the development of various allergic conditions. But the final word on this subject has not yet been said.

Extended discussion of the psychological appects of breast feeding is beyond the scope of this work. Many authorities claim that it helps to develop a warm bond between mother and child.

One of the arguments for breast feeding is the claim that it hastens the return to normal of the pelvic organs—the shrinking of the swollen uterus. There is no question that the act of nursing stimulates uterine contractions, which the woman can feel as "afterpains." Whether or not such contractions accelerate shrinking of the uterus is difficult to prove. When there is no infection or retained afterbirth, the uterus returns to normal size in six to eight weeks—with or without nursing.

The woman who undertakes to breast-feed her child assumes a risk that is negligible if she does not nurse: the risk of breast infection. In a very appreciable percentage of cases breast feeding is followed by cracking of the nipples; infection occurs, with pain, temperature, occasionally abscess formation, necessitating the discontinuance of nursing.

Susceptibility to infection is not due to any loss of aptitude on the part of our generation for breast feeding. It has always been a problem with nursing mothers. (Indeed, it is even a problem among domestic animals.) Even before the days when bacteria, the cause of infection, had been identified, the "caking of milk," as it was called, was recognized as a cause of fever. Actually, the fever is not due simply to a collection of milk—except for a brief rise in temperature at the time the veins of the breasts become tense and swollen with blood. The fever is due to an actual infection of the milk ducts.

If you want to nurse your baby, you should not be discouraged because you assume the risk of infection, any more than you should be discouraged from having children because you know the problems that children may bring with them. And such infections have absolutely no connection with future development of breast cancer.

But if you undertake breast feeding you should do so because you have a *genuine* desire for it. You should not be influenced by friends or relatives who proclaim it a duty of motherhood. For if you do undertake it, you must be willing to work at it seriously, to keep it up long enough to be worth while, both for yourself and your baby. This means a *minimum* of three months.

Under ideal circumstances, breast feeding makes for easier infant care—if you have sufficient milk and no supplementary formula is required. On the other hand, if you lack the patience to teach your baby to empty the breast properly, to wake your baby so that he sucks well during the time devoted to feeding, your breasts will produce less and less milk, your child will be tired from his efforts and yet unsatisfied. If this happens, he must be given a formula in addition, and may not do so well as on bottle feeding alone, while you experience all the disadvantages of both methods.

It should be stressed that—barring inadequate nipples, cracked nipples, or breast infection—a minimum of two weeks' trial is necessary to determine whether a sufficient supply of milk will develop to make breast feeding successful.

No type of examination can foretell that a woman *will* be entirely successful in breast feeding. The size of your breasts is in itself no guarantee. However, there are women in whom the breasts are obviously *not* sufficiently developed: The nipples are too small, are turned in, or do not become sufficiently erect on stimulation, so that the baby will not be able to suck well. It can almost be predicted that in these women attempts at breast feeding will meet with difficulty.

Nipple shields. In cases where the nipples are inadequate or need temporary protection nipple shields are used. As recently as the 1930's a common type of nipple shield was made of lead. It was felt that lead—because of its astringent nature—had some value in healing cracked nipples. These shields were abandoned because of evidence of lead poisoning in infants.

The nipple shields in use today are made of glass, with a

rubber nipple similar to that on a bottle. The glass shield is placed over the mother's breast, milk is extracted through the sucking action of the baby on the rubber nipple attached to the shield. This avoids direct contact in the case of a cracked nipple.

But the sucking action and the presence of moisture may continue to irritate the nipples. Usually, nursing does not proceed too successfully if a shield is required for any length of time.

Preparation of your nipples for nursing. Various techniques have been advocated to prepare the nipples as much as possible to withstand the rigors of nursing. One of these is gentle massage once or twice a day with some lanolin-containing cream during the last month of pregnancy. This is to stimulate the erection of the nipples and to soften the skin so that it will not crack so easily.

BEFORE GOING TO THE HOSPITAL

Hiring a baby nurse. Women who have been the eldest in a large family and helped raise infant brothers and sisters may face the trial of going home to assume the care of their own baby quite calmly. In this day of small families, however, such women are the exception. Most women feel oppressed by the tremendous weight of responsibility that is to fall upon them. And some do not feel physically up to the job of taking care of a baby full time for a week or two after leaving the hospital.

If you have a mother who is not only willing but *capable,* she can help to tide you over this difficult period—until your own self-confidence has developed and you feel strong enough. If you have to rely upon a professional baby nurse, it is best to try to obtain someone personally recommended by a friend or your doctor. For baby nurses vary in their ability to teach and inspire confidence in a new mother, and you are the one who will eventually have full charge of the baby.

Some nurses shut themselves off, with the attitude of "mustn't touch" as far as their little charge is concerned. You will be fortunate if you can find one interested in mother as well as infant, who can be careful without making you afraid that your baby is too delicate for you to handle.

How long it is desirable to have a nurse will depend upon your financial circumstances and your health. It is best to plan on having help for two weeks.

If yours is a second baby, and you feel confident of your ability to handle the new one, you may find it easier if someone takes care of the housework and prepares the meals while you care for the baby yourself.

WHAT TO HAVE READY FOR YOUR BABY

Get what you need early. Don't wait until the last minute to buy or borrow the various items you'll need to have waiting for you when you bring the baby home from the hospital. Remember that the expected date of delivery is just that: the *expected* date. Your baby may arrive early. And don't put off gathering what you'll need until after your baby comes. Some things will have to be ready for you when you return home. Even the items not needed immediately will be inconvenient to obtain for a while afterward. At first you may not feel up to shopping; after that all your time will be taken up by your new child.

If you expect your husband to purchase what is needed while you are still in the hospital, you may be disappointed. First of all, he'll want to spend his off-work hours seeing you and the baby. Second, he may not be able to obtain exactly what you had in mind for each item.

So do your shopping or borrowing early in the last months of pregnancy. If you do this, it won't be a hectic last-minute rush job. You'll be able to take your time, shop around enough to get exactly what appeals to you most, and really enjoy getting thing ready for your baby.

Furniture. First of all, your baby will need a *bed*. This is where he'll be spending most of his sleeping and waking hours for months to come. Almost anything that has sides to prevent the baby from falling out will serve as a bed: a clothes basket, a bassinet, or a crib. The most important thing is the mattress. It should be firm, flat, and smooth; it should fit inside the bed neatly, so there is no opening between the sides of the mattress and the inside of the bed in which the baby's arm or foot can get caught.

Next you will need facilities for bathing and changing the baby. A *bathinette* serves both purposes. You need a rust-proof bucket from which you can fill the bath and into which you can drain it. If you use a table top or bureau top instead of a bathinette, you'll need to put a thick pad or mattress under the baby when changing him; an enamelware, rubber, or plastic pan of sufficient size will serve as the baby's bathtub. Be sure that the surface on which you change and bathe the baby is high enough so that you don't have to stoop over very much, or you'll soon develop back and shoulder pains. Some women prefer to sit while attending to the baby, but most find this less convenient than standing.

For the baby's room there should be a *chair* in which you will be comfortable while feeding the baby. Your arm can get quite tired while holding the baby, so be sure the chair has arms on which to rest your elbow and is low enough so that your knees are raised as an added support.

It is helpful to have a *small table* next to this chair, to set the bottle on while burping the baby.

You'll also need a *chest of drawers* for your baby's things, and a *pail* for soiled diapers.

For the bed. You'll need:

Rubber sheets (4). Two should be large enough to cover the mattress completely and tuck under its sides. The other two can be small.

Crib pads (4). These are placed on top of the rubber sheets to absorb moisture when the baby spits up or wets.

Or: *flannel-backed rubber sheets* (4). These serve the purposes of both the rubber sheets and the pads together, are easy to wash, and dry quickly.

Sheets (5). These should cover the mattress and tuck well under the sides. If the mattress is small enough, diapers will serve very well as sheets.

Blankets (3). The kind of blankets you get depends on the weather. They should not be so heavy that they overheat the baby or make him uncomfortable. It is probably best to get two wool blankets and one cotton one as starters.

For bathing the baby. Close to the bathinette or dressing table you'll need:

Towels (4). These should be soft, thick, absorbent, and large enough to wrap completely around the baby.

Washcloths (4). Get two with a design on them, two that are plain. This will make it easier for you to remember which one you are using to clean the baby's face, which is for his body.

Baby soap.

Baby shampoo.

Baby oil.

Baby powder.

Lotion.

Ointment. A jar for diaper or heat rashes.

Box of sterile cotton.

Sterile cotton balls.

Swabs.

Sterile gauze pads.

Cotton receiving blankets (2).

Baby's tray. This is convenient for holding soap, cotton, swabs, and oil.

Rectal thermometer (infant's).

Baby's comb and brush.

For feedings. If you are breast feeding your baby, you will need only two or three *eight-ounce bottles* and a few nipples. You need these for feeding the baby water and juice, and they are handy to have around in case you have to give the baby a supplementary formula.

If you are not nursing your baby, you'll need:

Eight-ounce bottles (7). Ordinarily you'll be giving the baby six bottles a day, but since you are bound to break some it is wise to have an extra one handy.

Four-ounce bottles (2). For water and juice.

Nipples (9).

Bottle caps or glass nipple covers (7).

Brush. For cleaning bottles and nipples.

Sterilizer.

Funnel.

Strainer.

Measuring spoons.

Quart measure (enamelware or Pyrex). For mixing formula. Get one with measurements clearly marked.

Bottle tongs. For lifting bottles out of sterilizer.

Nipple jar. This should have a screw-on top with holes punched in it for sterilizing nipples.

Can opener.

Bibs (5).

For out-of-doors. Be sure you test the *carriage* before buying it. It should be light enough for you and easy to turn, balanced so that it will resist tipping. It is a good idea to get a transparent plastic *carriage cover* that shields the baby from strong winds.

Baby bag. For carrying diapers, cotton, a bottle, etc., when you take the baby out. A bag that can be slung from your shoulder by a long strap leaves both your hands free at all times.

Car crib.

Your baby's clothes. The first consideration, of course, is *diapers.* You'll need *at least* three dozen large ones, or you'll be constantly washing and drying them. The more you get, the less often you'll have to launder them.

If you arrange for a *diaper service* that supplies and launders them for you, it is still a good idea to buy a dozen extra diapers of your own for emergencies.

Safety pins (4). Special diaper safety pins that "lock" when closed will save you from worrying about the possibility of a pin opening by accident and sticking your baby.

Waterproof panties (4). These go over the diapers and save you from having to change the sheets and baby's clothes each time he wets.

Shirts (4). Short sleeves or sleeveless, depending on the weather and season. The kind that snap in front are easier to put on the baby at first (while he cannot co-operate with you, and is likely to squirm vigorously) than those that pull over the head.

Nightgowns (4). They should be long enough so that the baby's feet will not be exposed when he kicks.

Booties (1 pair).

Sweaters (2).

Bonnet or wool cap. For taking the baby out in cool weather.

WHAT TO TAKE TO THE HOSPITAL

For yourself. Pack the bag you intend to take to the hospital well in advance of the date your baby is due. If you have to do it hurriedly at the last moment you are bound to get upset and forget some things.

Your basic needs will be provided by the hospital. But here are some items you may wish to take along to make your stay more comfortable and enjoyable:

Nightgowns or pajama tops.

Bed jacket.

Bathrobe.

Bedroom slippers.

Sanitary belt and sanitary pads.

Tissues or handkerchiefs.

Toothbrush and toothpaste.

Cosmetics, talcum powder, and cologne.

Mirror, comb, and brush.

Stationery, fountain pen, and stamps.

Address book with addresses and phone numbers of friends and relations.

Sealed envelope containing soap flakes or powder for washing your stockings and underthings.

Magazines and books (light reading, preferably humorous).

For the baby. You'll want these things for taking the baby home:

A few diapers.

Waterproof panties.

Shirt.

Nightgown (or you may prefer a petticoat and pretty dress for the baby's first homecoming).

Safety pins (2).

Bonnet.

Blanket. (If the weather is cold, take several blankets and a sweater.)

PART III

Birth

CHAPTER 12

Birth Begins

WHEN WILL YOUR PREGNANCY END?

The date of full-term labor. At the time of your first visit to the obstetrician he gives you a date on which your baby may be expected. This date is usually arrived at by adding seven days to the date your last period started and counting back three months. This applies only when menstruation has been normal. A woman whose menstrual cycles were regularly about six weeks probably produced an egg and became pregnant two weeks later than the woman whose cycles were four weeks. The obstetrician may make a correction on this basis.

There may be a miscalculation if you had an apparently normal menstrual period after you had already conceived. If this happened, you would actually be due to deliver a month earlier than would be calculated on the basis of this false menstrual period. Allowance in this case will be made as soon as the obstetrician suspects that your pregnancy is further advanced than the date would indicate. Clues to this would be furnished by the more rapid growth of your uterus and from the date on which your baby's movements were first felt or its heartbeat first heard.

In any case, *no matter how regular* your menstrual periods have been, no matter how certain you may be of the very night or hour at which you conceived, the date given for the arrival of your baby can be only an approximation—an informed guess. It is subject to revision at any time during the last month. Even then labor may come on when it appears unlikely, or be delayed two or three weeks after everything points to its imminent onset.

Because the date given by the obstetrician represents the end of the ninth month, women tend to feel that it should indicate the *very last* day on which their baby can be expected to arrive. A full month earlier, as soon as they are in the ninth month, their hopes begin to rise. By the time the date given by the obstetrician is reached, they already feel they have been waiting overlong for labor to begin. With the help of friends and relatives, with the phrase "are you still around" ringing in their ears, anxiety may reach a disturbing and entirely unnecessary intensity.

Actually, the date calculated by the obstetrician represents the median position—*neither* the earliest a full-term baby can be expected, *nor* the latest. About 80 per cent of infants will be born within ten days earlier—or later—than the date given. Just as many will arrive later as earlier.

"Overdue" labor and post-maturity. (For prematurity, see page 202.) A problem develops when a woman goes far beyond the calculated date of delivery. For the obstetrician, the problem is twofold: He must decide whether there was an error in calculating the date; if there seems to be no error, he must decide how long it is safe to allow pregnancy to continue beyond full term before there is danger of developing a condition known as "post-maturity."

The post-mature baby is one that remains in the uterus so long beyond the normal time that it begins to suffer the effects of inadequate nutrition and inadequate oxygen supply —because the placenta becomes "too old" to do its job properly.

In post-maturity, the fluid that surrounds the baby starts to be reabsorbed. The baby seems to cease growing and may even appear smaller. Such post-mature infants, when delivered, often have a starved, emaciated appearance.

Various authorities have given different lengths of time to be accepted as the normal limit of pregnancy. In general, it is felt that continuation of pregnancy for three weeks beyond full term should lead to concern about post-maturity.

Once the calculated date of arrival has passed, the question arises as to whether to induce labor. At one time the only fear was that the baby would grow excessively large and therefore make for a very difficult delivery. This probably does not occur very often in the true post-mature case. As has been explained, the post-mature baby seems to cease growing. If the baby *is* still growing, it is not suffering from the effects of post-maturity. Obviously its nutrition must be quite adequate. And if the baby is still growing, it is not likely that inducing labor a week or so earlier will make the difference between a normal and an abnormal delivery. (See Induced Labor, page 199.)

But if the baby is *not* apparently growing after the due date has been passed, the obstetrician must decide when it is wiser to induce labor than to allow the pregnancy to continue. If his examination reveals that the neck of the womb is already thinned out and a little bit open, if the uterine muscle contracts upon stimulation, the obstetrician will usually try to induce labor, for these signs indicate that labor is ready to begin, and needs only to be started.

When, however, examination indicates that the ordinary methods of induction are not likely to succeed, the obstetrician is faced with another decision. He must decide whether to send the woman home for a further period of waiting, to resort to more drastic means of induction, or to perform a Caesarean section.

In the woman under the age of thirty there is usually very little risk in allowing pregnancy to continue as long as a full three weeks beyond the calculated date—if pelvic measurements indicate that she has a good chance of a normal delivery when labor does ensue. But in women beyond thirty-five—with a *first* baby—the risk of post-maturity becomes much greater. If labor cannot be induced, a Caesarean may be preferable to waiting for labor to start naturally, even when the pelvis appears adequate.

It must be stressed that there are no simple and obvious rules to guide an obstetrician in handling these problems. Such a multitude of impressions influence his decision— the feel of the uterus, the age of the patient (not in terms of years, but in physiology), etc.—that his final judgment as to whether or not the baby is thriving seems to come from a sixth sense.

HOW LABOR BEGINS

Pre-labor contractions. It is not possible to say in advance just how labor will begin for each woman. In many cases it is not possible to say that it has even *had* a definite beginning.

Throughout the last months of pregnancy there will be times when you are aware of a tightening of the uterus, a hardening of your whole abdomen. This is known as a contraction. As labor approaches, these contractions may occasionally become so strong that you are aware of a dull, crampy sensation accompanying them. The points to which these sensations are referred may vary as widely as the points to which menstrual discomforts are referred. Some women will feel them in the lower part of the abdomen, in the bladder region; others will feel them mostly low in the back, almost at the tip of the spine. Still others may feel them in the groin, sometimes radiating down into the thighs.

In the last few days before real labor begins these mildly painful contractions may become almost regular. When an attempt is made to time the interval between them, it will vary from twenty minutes to a half-hour to ten minutes. But eventually they will subside as you get bored with timing them and go about some other business or go to sleep.

These contractions have been given the name of "Braxton-Hicks," after the Englishman who originally described them. Although they are typically painless, the occasional contraction or group of contractions may be strong enough to register a certain amount of pain.

These contractions serve to *prepare* the lower portion of the uterus for labor. During the last weeks of pregnancy the portion of the uterus known as the cervix becomes very much thinner. It actually flattens out and begins to open slightly. The lowermost portion of the uterus also elongates and becomes thinner. Thus, the muscular contractions, instead of pressing equally on all parts of the baby, come to press in a *downward* direction. It is as though one were compressing a sack that is open or weakest at the lower end. The contractions now cause pressure on three sides of the baby, with no equal pressure from below. Each contraction will have the tendency to force the baby down toward the opening of the womb. This opening will eventually dilate enough to allow the baby to pass through.

There is tremendous variation as to how much discomfort women feel with these pre-labor contractions. In general, they are proportional to the amount of discomfort that they had during their menstrual periods. If your periods were painful, it indicates that you are normally very sensitive to contractions of the uterus.

There is no limit—even for a woman who has had children before—as to how long these preliminary contractions may come and go before definite labor begins. I have seen cases with definite contractions, registering as pains, as often as every five minutes during the last two months of pregnancy —till finally the expected date was reached—and passed.

Labor does not have a very definite beginning in all cases. Contractions may become quite strong for a period of hours, and yet subside gradually before you feel it is necessary to call the doctor. Nevertheless, if you have been examined before and after this period of stronger contractions, some definite progress in the opening and thinning of the lower portion of the uterus might have been detected—just as if you had been in actual labor. There is only one difference between these periods of stronger contractions and true labor: labor is a continuous process, terminating only with the birth of a child.

Eventually these contractions achieve a regular pattern. If you have a sensitive uterus, and have been aware of contractions on many days preceding, it may be difficult to decide just at what moment this more regular pattern has developed. This is not too serious a problem. You are in communication with your doctor, and he will be able to decide—from his personal knowledge of you, as well as from the combination of signs and symptoms—when it is time for you to go to the hospital.

Most women have a fear of going to the hospital too early. The obstetrician, on the other hand, merely wants to be sure that you are *really* in labor, because he wants you to be spared the disappointment of going back home undelivered. But he does *not* expect you to calculate things so carefully that you will spend only an hour or two in the hospital before the baby is born.

The mucus plug. Certain signs—besides increasing regularity of pains—frequently accompany the onset of true labor.

One of these is known as the mucus plug—a thick and stringy discharge—which is squeezed out of the neck of the womb as it thins out in preparation for labor. By itself it has little significance. It may appear many days before true labor commences. But if it appears in conjunction with fairly regular cramps, it is further evidence of real labor.

The bloody show. Often this sign will appear without any pains—as just a blood-streaked mucus discharge. In this case it has little significance, particularly if it appears shortly after a visit to the obstetrician and an internal or rectal examination was performed. If, however, this blood-tinged mucus appears in conjunction with crampy abdominal pains, it is good evidence that this is the real labor.

Rupture of the bag of waters. A sudden gush of clear water from the vagina, with an odor resembling semen, means that the membranes (the bag of waters) have ruptured. In almost every case labor will follow this within a matter of hours, *if you are at full term.* When the bag of waters ruptures *prematurely,* labor still may not come on for days—or, in rare cases, for weeks.

CALLING THE DOCTOR

When to call the doctor. Obstetricians wish to be called if there is an appreciable showing of blood, or if there is a gush of fluid indicating that the bag of waters has ruptured. Occasional and fleeting pains are not worth calling him about. In many cases they will simply disappear. But when abdominal cramps—fairly uniform in intensity and occurring regularly at intervals of not longer than ten minutes—continue for an hour or so, your doctor will wish to be notified.

This does not mean that if mild pains occur in the middle of the night you should make heroic efforts to stay awake in order to time them. If you are able to fall asleep, you are not in labor.

These suggestions concerning the onset of labor apply to the average case—particularly a first baby. If this is your second baby, and the labor with your previous one was only a few hours (or if it started off with exceptionally mild pains and then suddenly made rapid progress), your obstetrician may wish to be notified at a very much earlier stage, even when your pains are still irregular.

In some special cases—even with a first baby—your obstetrician may have reason to wish you to call him at the very first sign of labor: a stain, a leaking of fluid, or mild and irregular cramps. If so, he will make this very clear to you beforehand.

If you would do your doctor a favor, try to be the exceptional woman, and give him a *firsthand* description of your labor pains. Too often it is a male voice that the doctor hears on the phone in the middle of the night, announcing that his wife is in labor. Questions and answers are relayed through this husband, resulting in utter confusion.

It is not that the woman has been so incapacitated by pain that she is no longer capable of dialing a telephone, but that her husband is the more anxious of the two. His wife insists that these pains are very mild, and certainly cannot be the real thing. She doesn't want to disturb the doctor for nothing in the middle of the night. To which the husband replies: "If you won't call him, I will!"

The average woman receives twelve to fifteen hours' advance notice before the baby arrives. Some women may have preliminary cramps lasting two or three days, and still have a very normal labor when it finally develops. Other women may suddenly be seized by regular contractions coming at five-minute intervals or less, and then give birth within a very few hours. But it is the rare case where a baby is delivered within three hours of the first labor pain—whether it is a first baby or not. Such a labor is considered abnormally quick. It is classified obstetrically under the name of "precipitate labor."

The signs and symptoms of labor will of course have been discussed with your doctor many times during the last weeks of pregnancy. He will instruct you about how and when he wishes to be called. The timing or nature of the pains that he considers sufficient to warrant a call may be modified by external factors such as distance from the hospital, traffic conditions, or other difficulties of travel.

How to call the doctor. Women worry needlessly about reaching the doctor when their time comes. Obstetricians are, of course, conscious of their responsibilities in this regard. They make certain that their telephones are covered twenty-four hours a day. A call to the office at any hour of the day or night will be relayed promptly.

Many obstetricians have, in addition, a radio-paging service

—a little pocket-radio device with a code number assigned to each subscriber. If the doctor is out of reach of the telephone—in his car or at the beach, for example—he will be notified via radio that a call is waiting.

Naturally, the phone-answering service and the radio-paging service will not instantly relay calls from patients who simply call up to make an appointment. It is up to you to stress the fact that your call is *urgent*. Tell the operator that you are starting labor, so that your doctor will be contacted at once.

CHAPTER 13

Labor and Delivery

THE THREE STAGES OF LABOR

First stage. Obstetricians have divided labor into three stages. The first takes place entirely within the body, and consists of the gradual opening of the mouth of the uterus (called the cervix). When this opening—which may scarcely admit the tip of a finger at the onset of labor—dilates sufficiently to allow the baby's head to pass through, the first stage is over.

Second stage. Once this internal obstruction is overcome, the second stage of labor begins. Now your body, through contractions of the abdominal muscles—the so-called "bearing-down" efforts—starts to attempt to force the baby out through the vagina. When the baby is in a position to breathe, it is legally considered born. In other words, in a headfirst delivery the baby is born as soon as the head is delivered. In a breech delivery, the baby is not considered born until practically all of it is out. The delivery of the baby completes the second stage of labor.

Third stage. Now all that remains is the afterbirth (placenta), that normally has remained attached to the lining of the uterus until the birth of the child—and for a varying interval afterward. The uterus contracts down immediately to a fraction of its size as it becomes emptied of the child that lay within it. This may have the effect of immediately squeezing the afterbirth off the lining and into the cavity of the uterus. From there it may be expelled either by pressure from above (the voluntary bearing-down efforts on your part), or it may be removed manually by the obstetrician.

THE FIRST STAGE OF LABOR

The onset of labor. As was stressed before, the onset of
the first stage of labor may be so gradual, with vague pains
over a period of days, that it is impossible to tell—even in
retrospect—at exactly what moment it began. In other cases
the onset may be relatively sudden, with strong pains five
minutes or less apart.

The nature of the pains experienced will vary tremendous-
ly among different women. Generally, the early pains are felt
just above the pubic bone in the bladder region. Each time
the uterus contracts, you will feel the contraction as a hardening of your entire abdomen. You will experience a dull
pain down low in front, over the bladder. This tends to ra-
diate to your sides, to your groin, and down into your
thighs.

As your contractions progress and your cervix really begins
to dilate, the pain is usually (though not always) referred
to your back, near the base of the spine. Then the pains will
seem completely to encircle your body, the cramps either
spreading from the front to the back, or from the back forward. There is usually an increased amount of vaginal discharge at this time in the form of a thick mucus—with or
without tinges of blood.

Your water may or may not break this early. If it does
break early, even before the labor pains have been established, this does not mean any special difficulty (the so-
called "dry birth"). In fact, in most cases labor progresses
quite rapidly after the water bag ruptures.

The character of the pains, once they have definitely become established, does not tend to vary too greatly. But their
intensity and frequency do increase. Just how severe these
pains become cannot be predicted for any individual woman.
Some women—with or without special training for natural childbirth—will find such pains quite tolerable. Others—
even with training and understanding of natural childbirth,
and with the desire to co-operate—will say that these first-
stage pains (at least toward the end) were more difficult to
endure than the actual birth of the baby.

Hospital routine. Generally, by the time the pains are regular—somewhere between five and ten minutes apart—you

will be instructed to go to the hospital. Do not eat anything before leaving your home, and don't stop for a bite on the way. Your stomach should be empty before delivery.

Reception at the hospital varies according to different hospital routines. In some hospitals you will be separated from your husband in the admitting office and taken directly to a labor room. In others, you are taken to your own room —the room that you are to occupy throughout your stay in the hospital—and your husband is allowed to join you after the preliminary preparations for labor have been taken care of.

Most hospitals keep the husband in the admitting office long enough to obtain a history—which includes information about relatives, nationality, etc. It is also generally the custom of all hospitals to request, at the time of admission, a deposit equal to the estimated cost of the hospital stay. If you have Blue Cross insurance, allowance is made for this, and it is deducted.

You will not usually be detained in the admitting office, especially if you show any signs of being uncomfortable. You will be taken immediately to the maternity floor. There you will undress and go to bed in a short hospital gown. The first thing to which you must submit is the shaving of all hair around the vagina and rectum. This is in the interests of sterility and proper healing following delivery.

Then, if labor is not too advanced, it is generally considered advisable to administer a cleansing enema. The purpose of this is twofold. First of all, it frequently will stimulate your contractions and accelerate the labor. In the second place, when your child is about to be born, the involuntary and voluntary expulsive efforts cause pressure on the rectum as well as on the child to be born. In the interests of sterility, it is well to have the rectum empty.

You may be annoyed at this time to find the water pitcher in the room empty and no one volunteering to fill it. The reason for this is that every woman in labor, no matter what the plans for delivery, may need anesthesia for one reason or another. There is nothing more dangerous than to administer a general anesthetic upon a full stomach. Therefore, no food or drink is given to a woman in active labor, if it is thought that delivery within a matter of six hours is a possibility.

It is for this reason—particularly with second and subsequent babies, where labor may be expected to be rapid—that you should not stop to eat before going to the hospital, even if the pains are mild and you feel hungry.

Following the enema you can expect frequent visits from the nurses in charge of the labor room, from the staff doctors and, of course, from your own physician. You may be a little annoyed that each will place a hand on your abdomen and feel qualified to judge the intensity of the pain you are feeling. Often, when you think a pain has been quite severe, someone will say, "Oh, that wasn't much of a pain." In other cases you may be rewarded for what you have felt by hearing, "That was a particularly *good* pain"—and be encouraged to know that labor is progressing.

There are two aspects to labor pains. First, the amount of discomfort that you feel. Second, the strength of the contractions of the uterus, which is judged by what the doctor or nurse feels when placing a hand on your abdomen at the time you are experiencing the pain. To the doctor or nurse the "quality" of the pain is measured only by how hard the uterus feels and how long the contraction lasts.

You may be surprised that your doctor can tell the coming of a pain before you yourself are aware of it. He is able to feel the tightening of the uterus before it reaches sufficient intensity to register in your own mind as a pain.

The intensity and frequency of labor pains are something of a guide to the progress of labor. Very often this has been so impressed upon couples that by the time the doctor visits the room he will find written out on a long sheet of paper the exact time and duration of every labor pain the woman has experienced. It is eagerly brought to his attention as if he could make some exact prediction after studying it. Usually, where the husband is allowed to remain in the room with his wife, he is seen sitting in a chair, a watch in one hand and a pencil in the other, keeping this accurate record. Actually, it is no longer very useful when you are safely in the hospital. It serves, probably, as the modern equivalent of sending the husband to boil water—to give him something to do.

More accurate knowledge of the progress of labor must be obtained through rectal or vaginal examinations. Rectal examination is simpler because no sterile precautions are necessary, since nothing is introduced into the vagina. It is almost as accurate as vaginal examination, because only a thin layer of tissue separates the vagina from the rectum. Through the wall of the rectum the doctor is able to feel how far open the mouth of the uterus has become. He can also feel how far the lowermost part of the baby (which is known as the "presenting" part) has descended, and whether it is a headfirst or a breech position. In a headfirst position, it is useful to know which way the head is turning.

When the presentation is abnormal, and more direct information is desirable, the doctor may perform a vaginal examination. To prevent introduction of bacteria, such examinations must be performed with all sterile precautions. Antiseptic is sprayed about the vaginal opening, or painted on. The doctor scrubs up, puts on sterile gloves, cap, and mask, just as if he were going to perform an operation in the operating room.

Relief from labor pains. At some time during the first stage of labor most women will feel that they would like some relief from the intensity of the labor pains. No matter what method of pain relief is used, it cannot, unfortunately, always be given to best advantage as soon as the woman requests it. No method can produce its best effects unless labor has progressed sufficiently first. Just how far it must progress depends upon the judgment of the individual doctor for the individual woman. No arbitrary rule can be laid down.

It is at this stage of labor that the factors stressed by the advocates of natural childbirth have their greatest application. Your surroundings should be pleasant and reassuring, for it is anxiety, more than anything else, that increases the need for very early use of pain-relieving measures.

With most forms of medication a doctor will prefer to wait until there is good prospect of delivery within four to six hours. With second or third babies, this may be almost as soon as the woman reaches the hospital. But with the first baby, women often come to the hospital with practically no progress beyond that which had been observed in the doctor's office on the last visit. It may be a matter of several hours before medication can be given with the assurance that labor will progress satisfactorily.

Normally, in the case of a first baby, the obstetrician will want to wait till the neck of the womb (the cervix) has been completely thinned out and is open at least the breadth of two fingers. When it is not the first baby, he must be guided by the character of the pains and the speed of previous deliveries.

As for the methods of relieving pain during childbirth, everything has been used—including whisky, spinal anesthesia, and hypnotism.

"Twilight sleep." Probably the most popular method of relieving pain during childbirth today consists of a combination of drugs that produces a light plane of anesthesia popularly known as "twilight sleep." Ideally, it is possible to maintain a woman in this condition for about six hours with perfect safety for herself and the baby. While under twilight sleep you sleep soundly between contractions. When the contractions are not too severe, you will stir only slightly with them. Later, your behavior will depend more or less on the degree of anxiety.

A calm, confident person will change position with the pains, may rouse enough to talk incoherently, sometimes holding lengthy imaginary conversations with persons who are not there. The woman who is very apprehensive may cry out with the pains, occasionally making violent attempts to get out of bed. For that reason, when this form of medication is administered, you must be in a bed with criblike sides to prevent you from falling out and hurting yourself. You must be under constant observation. It is because women have been heard to cry out in this condition—and then remember nothing about it later—that some regard very dubiously this method of pain relief. They say: "Is that the method where you feel all the pain, only you can't remember it?"

Hypnotism. Hypnotism has been regarded as everything from a form of entertainment to the greatest medical discovery of the age. Everyone has read accounts of women who have gone through childbirth under its influence.

There is no doubt that a hypnotic trance can produce complete anesthesia to any form of pain. The point to be remembered is that there is no such thing as a hypnotist; there are only people capable of hypnotizing themselves. They tell themselves a thing is so, and the hypnotist merely helps them to believe it.

The essence of hypnosis is the ability to withdraw one's attention from his immediate surroundings. Every woman who has spoken to her husband, only to receive a mechanical and irrelevant reply, followed much later by "What did you say?" must realize that a minor trance is easily induced.

But *very few* are capable of achieving a state that can resist painful stimulation.

Anesthetics. Inhalation anesthetics are also used to relieve pain in the first stage of labor. At one time whiffs of chloroform were given with each pain. This has been abandoned because of occasional poisoning. Nitrous oxide or laughing gas is safe to use in this manner but requires cumbersome apparatus.

At the present time the only anesthetic used at all widely for this purpose is trilene. This volatile liquid is contained in a small apparatus through which the woman breathes each time she feels a pain coming on. It rapidly produces a numbness to pain without loss of consciousness.

Saddle block. All anesthetic agents, the drugs of twilight sleep—even hypnosis—relieve pain by their effect on the highest centers of the brain, where pain registers on our consciousness. It is also possible to block the nerve pathways by which painful stimuli reach these centers of the brain. This is known as "conduction anesthesia." There are various forms of conduction anesthesia, all of which possess in common the advantage of not affecting the baby.

Saddle block is a form of spinal anesthesia. The anesthetic drug is injected into the fluid surrounding the spinal cord. It differs from ordinary spinal anesthesia in that it is injected with the patient sitting up, and the drug is dissolved in liquid made heavy by addition of sugar. This causes the anesthetic to remain concentrated at the lowest level of the spinal cord, which receives nerves from the pelvic region. Thus the level of anesthesia does not rise above the navel, yet pain of labor and birth is abolished.

The disadvantages of this form of anesthesia are that it lasts only two to three hours, and that it may be followed by "spinal headache." This is a throbbing headache recurring for days whenever the patient sits up. It can follow any spinal tap.

Caudal anesthesia. During World War II caudal anesthesia aroused the greatest enthusiasm as the final answer to obstetrical pain. Technically it is more difficult to administer than spinal anesthesia. The needles must find a small opening in the bone at the base of the spine that is little larger in diameter than the needle itself. This leads to a space below the spinal cord and its surrounding fluid, where the nerves emerge in a bunch (like the tail of a horse, which is the meaning of its Latin name, *cauda equina*).

A pliable needle or plastic tube may be taped in place so that further doses of anesthetic may be injected as needed, maintaining anesthesia for many hours. The extent of anesthesia is similar to that obtained with "saddle block," abolishing labor pains and anesthetizing the area about the vagina and the rectum.

But there are disadvantages to caudal anesthesia. Because of technical difficulty it is not always successful. It is not considered wise to administer it until the cervix is more than two finger breadths dilated. By this time other drugs may have been required for relief which can comfortably and safely carry the woman over the few hours remaining.

Headache does not follow caudal anesthesia, since the needle remains outside the sac containing spinal fluid. However, in some individuals this sac extends to an abnormally low level and may be accidentally entered, producing spinal rather than caudal anesthesia. The method is not without its dangers and must be administered by an expert.

Local nerve block. The nerves that transmit sensations from the vaginal area may be anesthetized with novocaine just as the dentist blocks nerves for tooth extraction. This renders delivery of the baby and "stitching" painless, but affords no relief from labor pains.

How long a labor? It is hard to say how long the first stage of labor may last because of the difficulty of determining exactly what constitutes the beginning. Two women, in comparing labors, may give entirely different versions. One may say she was in labor for two days, the other that she was in labor for six hours. Yet if you go into details, you find that they both experienced exactly the same thing. The first woman considered the earliest cramps the beginning of her labor; the other disregarded all cramps until they became severe enough to warrant her going to the hospital.

Most of the very long labors you hear about represent nothing more serious than going to the hospital too soon—perhaps a day or more earlier than necessary. Far fewer women would fall into this error if left alone in their judgment, for their concern is more often with the possibility of false alarm. It is generally the husband who becomes too nervous to allow his wife to remain at home with any type of labor pains.

The textbooks give the average labor—which is largely this first stage of labor—as twelve to fifteen hours for a first baby and about eight hours for subsequent babies. Here—as with women's calculations of their own labors—the estimate may be colored by the decision of the author as to what he is willing to consider a genuine labor pain.

By medical standards a "prolonged" labor is defined as one lasting more than thirty hours. We rarely encounter true labors of this length today—if we consider labor as beginning with definite progress in dilation of the cervix. As was stressed before, there is no limit to the duration of *preliminary* cramps before progressive dilation takes place.

If dilation has definitely taken place, and then proceeds to slow down greatly, most obstetricians feel justified in stimulating the contractions to speed the conclusion of labor. Even with first babies, labor of more than ten hours is unusual.

The variation in the time consumed in the first stage of labor depends on a number of factors—not all of which are clearly understood. The most effective labor appears to be in women in their twenties. The very young, contrary to popular notions, do not fare quite so well. The sixteen- and seventeen-year-olds, on the average, tend to have somewhat more difficult labors. And women having first babies after the middle thirties should anticipate slower progress.

The extremely obese will tend to have slower and less effective labor pains. The roominess of your pelvis may also play a part. However, the dilation may proceed rapidly, even though delivery from below proves impossible because of narrow bone structure. Ineffective labor pains and poor pelvic architecture do not *necessarily* go hand in hand. Position of the baby may also be a factor. If the baby lies across the mother's abdomen, or in other unusual positions that prevent a portion of it from entering the cervix as a firm dilating wedge, progress is likely to be poor.

Psychological factors unquestionably can play a role in the progress of the first stage of labor. Just as the movements of the intestines are beyond our command to accelerate or slow down, so the contractions of the uterus are outside your voluntary control. But strong emotion can affect the frequency and vigor of the contractions of the uterus, just as they may affect the involuntary contractions of the intestinal tract. Diarrhea following a severe fright is not just a figure of speech.

There is a popular notion that the more athletic woman will have a speedier labor and easier childbirth. Experience does not bear this out. It is frequently the entirely feminine, soft-muscled type whose labors are remarkably fast. The husky woman who competes successfully with men on the athletic fields often falls far behind in competing with the members of her own sex on the labor bed. There is no relationship between the development of the skeletal muscles with which we perform our athletic feats and the development of the uterine muscle which hastens the birth of a baby.

There is another popular notion that it is the activity of the baby that somehow plays a part in hastening or retarding birth. When labor is long, you often hear relatives say that the baby must be a "lazy girl." Actually, the baby is strictly a passenger. It can do nothing to hasten or retard its birth. Its role is purely passive. The only time when the infant's activities may affect birth is if it somehow manages to get itself in an abnormal position that obstructs the progress of labor.

SECOND STAGE OF LABOR: DELIVERY

"Bearing down." The second stage of labor is ushered in when the uterus, by its own contractions, has succeeded in opening its lower end completely. The baby now enters into the vagina and begins to press, first, against the rectum, distending and opening the anus.

At this stage, even in a semi-conscious state, you react to a change in the character of your pains. The first-stage pains call for no special type of activity on your part; you might move from side to side restlessly, clench your fists, moan, or else go through some set pattern of breathing exercises designed to relax you and prevent tensing of muscles. But when the second-stage pains begin, you will find an almost uncontrollable desire to press, or "bear down," as though in the midst of a difficult bowel movement.

As you bear down, the first obvious sign that delivery is about to take place is the opening of your anus. It will open to the size of a half-dollar or silver dollar with each bearing-down pain. For this reason, if you were completely conscious at this stage of labor, you would have no sensation of something large about to come out of the vagina. Instead, you would feel exactly as if something huge were emerging from your rectum.

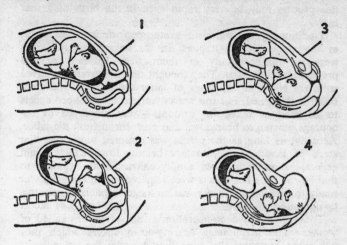

FIGURE D. How Your Baby Is Born

It is at this point that a woman under the influence of twilight sleep may become most difficult to control. Unless the depth of the anesthesia is very deep, the sensation penetrates to consciousness sufficiently to arouse the powerful fear—going back to the earliest days of toilet training—that she is about to soil the bed in which she lies. She becomes very restless every time she feels this sensation and will endeavor to get out of bed to go to the bathroom, since she is at this point not aware of what actually is taking place.

Duration of the second stage. The second stage of labor may be a very brief one in women who have had previous babies. The muscles surrounding the vagina and the vaginal opening, having previously been stretched, do not impede the progress of the baby for any appreciable length of time. Birth may take place in a matter of minutes, or even seconds, after the uterus is completely open.

With first babies, however, there is resistance of these muscles to be overcome. Frequently an hour or more may be necessary to allow the gentle stretching and relaxation of these muscles before delivery will take place spontaneously, or may be assisted safely with the use of forceps. There is great variation among individual women. For some of them this process may be very rapid even in the birth of a first baby.

Traditionally, giving birth meant performing hard work, as the name "labor" implies. In the days when midwives were in charge, many of them were ignorant of the processes taking place. They thought that if a woman exerted sufficient effort at *any* stage of labor the birth of the child could be hastened. For this reason various means—bed sheets to be used as reins, for example—were employed to encourage women to bear down and press throughout the labor. Actually, as long as the uterus was a closed sac in the first stage of labor, such voluntary bearing-down efforts could accomplish nothing. They simply exhausted the woman, so that by the time her efforts were required, when the baby was ready to be forced out, she was no longer capable of effective co-operation.

Today this active co-operation is not often demanded of women. The *involuntary* bearing-down efforts which they will make *automatically*, even though under the influence of twilight sleep, will be sufficient to force the baby out spontaneously—or to bring it down to a point where it can be safely assisted with forceps.

However, where there is more resistance to be overcome—where the pelvis is of borderline proportions, the baby large, or the head turned in a less normal position—the ability of the woman to co-operate, to press down with strength and endurance, may make the difference between a safe and relatively easy delivery and a difficult one for mother and infant. Fortunately these cases are rare. Probably 90 per cent of all women will be called upon only for brief efforts at this stage to make delivery easy.

Into the delivery room. Whenever the obstetrician decides that you are ready to give birth, you will be wheeled into the delivery room and transferred to the delivery table. Such tables vary considerably in detail, but the main features are the same. You lie on your back with your knees held up and apart by supporting devices known as stirrups. Try not to be annoyed if you are aware that your hands are held at your sides by some sort of cuffs about the wrists. Such restraints are always necessary when anesthesia is to be given.

Delivery tables are constructed so that the lower half

may be removed when everything is ready for delivery. Thus your buttocks come to lie at the very edge of the table.

The final aspect of the second stage of labor is actual stretching of the vaginal opening as birth is taking place.

Incisions and stitches. The first pressure of the baby's head was against the rectum. Now the head of the baby rises forward and begins to spread the vaginal opening. It is when about two to three inches of the surface of the baby's head are visible, as the vaginal opening distends, that the obstetrician usually makes up his mind whether to make the incision known as an "episiotomy." He can feel just how much elasticity is in the tissues, whether they have reached the limit to which they will stretch without some tearing taking place.

Many women are unduly concerned about "stitches" and the pain which they will cause. It is true that it is hard to reconcile a normal process such as birth with the almost universal practice of rendering it at least a minor surgical operation by the performance of an episiotomy. Nevertheless, there is strong evidence that this small operation does preserve better muscles for this portion of the woman's body. There is less likelihood later in life of a sagging of the internal organs, bulging of the bladder and rectum into the vagina, or the protrusion of the uterus outside the vagina. Such unfortunate results of childbirth would require plastic operations for their repair.

There are, of course, many women who—with patience and slow stretching—would find sufficient elasticity in their tissues to give birth to a moderate-sized baby without tearing the skin. However, rather than run the *risk* of a laceration that may be ragged and heal poorly, it is better to make a clean incision that is more easily repaired. The performance of episiotomy is considered a preventive, or "prophylactic," measure.

The incisions are of two main types. One incision is directly in the "midline," extending from the lowermost part of the vaginal opening directly back toward the opening of the rectum. This is the type most frequently made when the obstetrician feels that the baby will not be too large or delivery too difficult. This type of incision is preferred because the pull of the muscles is such that the incision comes together naturally. It requires very little tension from stitches to hold it in place. Healing is rapid, smooth, and the scar is practically invisible. The woman suffers a minimum of discomfort.

There is an objection to this type of incision when the baby is large, or the arch of bone under which the baby's head must pass is narrow, forcing it back toward the rectum. The midline incision may not make the opening large enough, even when extended to its maximum limit. Further stretching would cause the incision to tear in the same direction. This would extend the incision directly into the rectum itself. Such tears are not extremely dangerous. The women suffers no more discomfort than she would with the incision alone, and when competently repaired, healing is just as smooth. However, should any infection occur, so that healing did not take place properly, or should a stitch break down, a communication might be left between the vagina and the rectum. This permits leakage from the rectum into the vagina, requiring operative repair at a later date.

Therefore, as a safety measure, many obstetricians prefer to start their incision at the same place—the lowermost part of the vaginal opening—but to make the incision toward the side. This allows a longer incision. The entire distance from the vaginal opening to the rectal opening is little more than an inch when the tissues are not stretched. When the incision is made to the side, greater enlargement of the vaginal opening is possible. Also, if the incision is still inadequate and further tearing takes place, it does not enter into the rectum so readily.

One of the most frequent questions asked of an obstetrician following delivery is: "How many stitches did I have?" Obstetricians, in order to avoid lengthy explanations, may simply satisfy the new mother's curiosity with the casual figure of two, three, four, or five. But actually, measurement of this type of incision in terms of number of stitches does not have too much significance.

The ordinary skin incision can be measured in length by the number of stitches required to close it, because stitches placed through the skin are generally somewhere between a quarter-inch and a half-inch apart. The number of stitches is roughly proportional to the length of the incision. But the incision made at the birth of a child is not of this simple nature —that of a straight-line cut in the skin.

Instead, it is as though one had a triangular barrier to cut through. Stitches have to be placed, first, on the inside of the barrier—which corresponds to the inner lining of the vagina. Then stitches must be taken in the solid portion—the muscles and binding tissues. Finally, the outside—the skin—has to be brought together by stitches through the skin or beneath the skin.

The *skin* part of the incision probably does not vary more than a half-inch in length in 90 per cent of all deliveries performed. If the incision is made in the midline there is only a little more than an inch of skin that *can* be involved. But the vaginal part of the incision may be only an inch or two in length, or it may extend three or four inches into the vagina. It is closed by a continuous stitching much as one would baste a hem. Few doctors would have any notion of the number of stitches they have taken here. No matter what their number, these stitches *within* the vagina cause no discomfort.

As was mentioned before, these incisions are usually made only moments before the baby is actually delivered. In most cases, you would be under the influence of whatever anesthetic was being used and therefore would not be aware of the incision as it was being performed. Under conditions of "natural" childbirth, doctors infiltrate the skin with a novocaine solution so that if the incision is made it is quite painless. In cases where no anesthesia of any kind was administered, it has been found that as the tissues are stretched when the baby's head is about to deliver, they become rather numb. Even with no anesthesia at all, the tissues may be cut with less pain than one would imagine.

Birth. In the normal, spontaneous delivery, the baby is delivered through your efforts of bearing down, holding your breath, contracting your abdominal muscles just as if you were trying to have a very difficult and resistant bowel movement. Your efforts may be aided by the obstetrician or his assistant. He applies gentle but firm pressure on your abdomen in order to help your own muscular efforts. The obstetrician's attention is directed at this point mostly to controlling the rate at which the baby's head delivers, so that there is no sudden, violent expulsion that might cause extensive laceration.

As the baby's head extends, the obstetrician's hand—which is draped with a towel and pressed against the skin just behind your rectum—will feel the brow of the baby as a ledge which he can grasp. Once he has grasped this ledge, he can control the rate of delivery without any assistance on your part. If it is desired, you may now simply relax your bearing-down efforts and breathe deeply of the anesthetic.

The head delivers, normally, by extending. The chin of the baby is down on his chest as his head first appears at the outlet. The top of his head impinges against the arch of bone beneath which it must pass. At this point the head is allowed gradually to extend—first the brow appears, then the nose, and finally the chin.

The baby's head now turns to assume its normal position in relation to its body, which is still within you. In a majority of cases the baby's back lies toward the left. The obstetrician, by gentle traction, brings the baby's shoulder beneath your pubic bone and then lifts to free the other shoulder. Birth is now complete.

Forceps delivery. Not every woman will give birth by her bearing-down efforts alone. Many more could, however, if the obstetrician wished to make them continue bearing down long enough. In the case of the average first baby this would probably take somewhere between a half-hour and one hour from the time the baby's head first became visible at the vaginal opening.

But there is a question as to whether there is any advantage in continuing bearing down to effect this normal birth. Many obstetricians feel that assistance at this time with instruments not only spares the mother unnecessary effort, but is actually less injurious to the baby.

In the normal birth it is the baby's head itself which is the dilating wedge that stretches the vaginal opening. Many of these babies are born with greatly swollen scalps, with actual collections of blood over the bones of the skull. This is evidence of the force to which their heads have been subjected.

Forceps, on the other hand, exert pressure only on the sides of the baby's head, over the cheekbones. The skull, which is soft and flexible, and contains the brain, is spared excessive amounts of pressure. This does not mean, of course, that instruments should be used in all births. But there is no advantage to be gained in allowing the baby's head to be used as a battering ram for excessive lengths of time just in the hope that a "normal" delivery will result.

There are dozens of different types of forceps, many of which have special uses for special types of delivery. The principle of the forceps in greatest use today, however, remains the same.

Forceps consist of two separate "blades" of steel and have two types of curves. The first curve is shaped to the baby's head. The second curve follows the normal contour of a woman's pelvis. When these two blades are locked together, the curved parts of the two blades form an open pocket between them. It is inside the two curves of the blades that the baby's head fits.

It is as though you cupped your two hands, brought your wrists and the tips of your fingers together, and grasped an egg between your cupped palms. You could not squeeze the egg hard enough to break it unless you squeezed your palms together—which you could not do as long as you kept your hands cupped. The steel blades of the forceps, when locked together, form an oval around the baby's head and cannot be compressed further.

The two blades of the forceps are completely separate from each other until locked together. In delivering a baby, first one blade is slipped gently into position around the side of the baby's head. Then the other blade is slipped around the other side of the baby's head. *Then* the two parts of the forceps are joined, and locked together so that the baby can be assisted out of the mother's birth canal.

To understand this, again imagine your two hands as the two blades of the forceps. Cup each hand and keep them cupped rigidly. By sliding one hand around an egg, you can get a grip on one side of it. Then you slide the other hand around the other side of the egg. Then you bring the wrists together—keeping your hands still cupped. You will now have a grip upon the egg. You can exert pressure on the egg only by withdrawing your hands while keeping your wrists together. Thus you can pull the egg toward you. But as long as you keep your hands cupped and your wrists locked you cannot crush or compress the egg between your palms. If the egg were too large, you would not have been able to get your wrists together in the first place to lock them as forceps must be locked. And of course if the egg were too small, it would simply slip through your hands.

Forceps are designed to fit the size of any fully-developed infant's head. Special forceps are used when necessary for small, premature infants.

What has been said here does not mean, however, that

no damage can be done with forceps. If the delivery is extremely difficult, the tips of the forceps may cut into the baby's tissues in front of the ears, where they normally grasp. In some cases, where the head is fixed in an abnormal position in the pelvis and must be turned, the tips of the forceps may even cause injury to the mother. But this applies only to the *most difficult* cases, where it is a question of fine judgment as to whether delivery from below can be effected safely, or whether it would be better to perform a Caesarean section.

Women are always greatly concerned about their babies being marked by forceps. With normal amount of pressure against the delicate skin of the baby, a red mark will be visible temporarily—generally on the baby's cheek. This fades out rapidly. It never leaves a blemish of any sort.

Tending to the baby. Traditionally, completion of the birth is indication for a hearty slap upon the baby's buttocks to stimulate the long-awaited first cry. Actually, this practice is not very prevalent. Your baby, attached to its afterbirth (which still lies within your uterus), is laid upon your abdomen with its head lower than the rest of its body. This is so that the collection of fluid, mucus, and bloody discharge (from you) which is in the baby's mouth will have an opportunity to drain out.

A soft rubber tube with a glass mouthpiece may be used to suck fluid out of the baby's nose and throat. By the time your baby gives its first gasp, its air passages will be clear and it will not aspirate foreign material into its lungs. Thus, instead of trying to hasten that first gasp, the doctor actually prefers that several seconds pass to give him time to clear the baby's air passages.

Naturally, the suction itself, particularly if the tube is placed in the baby's nose, is usually sufficiently irritating to bring about a sneeze, a cough, and the first cry. No slap is necessary.

In any normal case the baby will usually cry within the first minute. Just what brings on the first cry is not conclusively proven. Possibly it is the change in temperature. The baby comes from the warmth of the mother to the relatively cool outside world. Babies actually do breathe—or at least make all the motions involved in breathing—while still inside the uterus, completely submerged in water. Possibly the air, filling the lungs, and now being forced out, is in itself a sufficient stimulus to bring on the cry. However, babies who have had their respiratory centers depressed have not breathed yet, and are blue from lack of oxygen, will still go through all the facial contortions associated with a cry —except that, since they are not breathing, no sound is possible.

Once the baby's air passages are cleared and the baby has cried, the next procedure is to cut the cord. This is usually done by applying two surgical clamps to shut off the flow of blood and cutting between them. The cord is composed of a gelatinous substance through which the artery and veins course. When it has been cut, the baby can be transferred to the bassinet.

At this point a special clamp may be applied, which is not so heavy as the surgical clamp and may be left in place for twenty-four hours, or until the cord drops off. But the most common practice is to tie the cord with material much like bias tape. One or two ties, according to the caution of the obstetrician, are placed, usually leaving three quarters to an inch of cord attached to the baby's navel. This shrivels up, becomes black and withered, and finally—sometime between the seventh and tenth day—will drop off.

THE THIRD STAGE OF LABOR

Expulsion of the placenta. To return to the mother. At this time the placenta (afterbirth) is still in the uterus. The cord, protruding from the vagina, has been clamped. If this clamp should be removed, there would be an escape of blood, but it would be the *baby's* blood, which has been left in the placenta and its vessels, and not your blood. This clamp is left in place only for purposes of neatness.

The time required for the placenta to separate spontaneously from its attachment to the lining of your uterus may vary from a few seconds to several hours.

Under natural conditions, where no anesthetic has been given, labor pains are not over with the birth of the child. The uterus contracts after delivery, and the woman lies quietly, resting for a few minutes. Then once again she feels cramps as the uterus begins to contract actively in an effort to expel the placenta, which has now separated itself.

Frequently this separation is accompanied by a trickle of

blood that has accumulated behind the placenta and now begins to escape. The placenta is squeezed out of the uterus by the force of the contractions. In the vagina it again causes a feeling of pressure, a desire to bear down as if to move one's bowels. Under these circumstances the expulsive efforts on the part of the mother would now give birth to the placenta, accompanied by a gush of blood.

Removal of the placenta. Today most women are under the influence of drugs or anesthetics after the baby is delivered. They are unaware of these sensations. The obstetrician, by feeling the position of the uterus, or by seeing the trickle of blood, is made aware of the time at which the placenta has separated. Placing his hand on the mother's abdomen and grasping the uterus—which has now come down to the level of the navel—and pressing gently, he is able to push out the placenta without any co-operation from the mother.

Abnormal cases, where there is excessive bleeding and the placenta cannot be expressed promptly, may require intervention by the obstetrician. The woman must be anesthetized so that he may insert his hand into the uterus. If the placenta has separated and is lying free within the uterus, he simply grasps it and removes it. In other cases only an edge of the placenta may have separated, allowing bleeding to take place; the rest of the placenta remains attached. This attachment is a loose one. The obstetrician can peel the placenta off the uterus, much as one would peel wet paper away from a surface to which it was adherent. Gentleness is of course required. It is desirable to remove this tissue in one piece, for if it is torn, it may be difficult to know whether all of it has been removed.

Even with the most skillful management, it is not possible to avoid the retention of fragments of placenta if they have been more firmly attached than normal to the wall of the uterus. It is unfair of women to talk about a doctor "leaving" placenta in them. Actually, there is no way a doctor can be entirely certain that all the placenta has come out. On the most careful examination the placenta may appear complete and yet a few days later a rather large portion may be expelled. No obstetrician would feel justified in exploring the uterus after a normal delivery merely to make certain that there were no fragments of afterbirth attached. The risk is too small to justify such a routine.

Retained fragments of placenta may be passed much later

with no difficulty. In other cases they may cause excessive bleeding even weeks after delivery. Occasionally, women have to return to the hospital for the minor operation of curettage—which is simply a scraping of the lining of the uterus to remove these fragments of afterbirth.

Once the placenta has been expressed and the incision repaired, the delivery is complete.

Bleeding and afterpains. It is often the practice to leave the mother in the delivery room for a half hour to an hour after delivery in order to make sure that the uterus remains firmly contracted. The mother's blood vessels have been closed by a network of contracting uterine muscle. If the uterus relaxes, the vessels will again open and hemorrhage take place. It is for this reason that you are under the constant supervision of the nurse. This careful observation continues for many hours after delivery. At any time in this period it is possible for the muscles of the uterus to relax and excessive bleeding occur. You will probably be given one or another of a combination of drugs that stimulate the firm contraction of the uterus. This prevents such bleeding. These drugs are either synthetic or natural extracts of ergot, or extracts of the posterior portion of the pituitary gland.

In the woman who has borne previous children it is normal for the uterus to relax slightly, and this relaxation is followed immediately by a stronger contraction. These contractions give rise to what are known as afterpains, or afterbirth pains. (For more on bleeding and afterpains, see page 219.)

CHAPTER 14

Delivery Complications

CAESAREAN SECTION

When are Caesarean operations performed? At the very first visit to their obstetricians, women want to know if they can have a baby normally or will need a Caesarean operation. Some have been made so fearful of the pains of normal labor that they are actually hopeful that they may have to have this method of delivery, "like the movie stars." Others take the opposite view. Influenced by stories from the past—when the Caesarean operation carried much more danger than it does today—they regard the possibility with exaggerated fear.

The obstetrician will rarely know at the first visit whether or not a Caesarean will be necessary. The measurements which he takes at that time tell something of the size but little of the shape of the pelvic passage through which the baby is born. They can tell him nothing of the size of the baby you are destined to have, the position in which it will come to lie at the time of delivery, or the efficiency with which your uterus will function.

As you enter your ninth month, and the time approaches when delivery may be expected, your obstetrician endeavors as best he can to determine the adequacy of your pelvic passage for the size of your baby. This is done by internal examination and by the taking of X rays using special techniques so that the distorted shadows that are cast on the X-ray film may be translated into terms of absolute measurement. But factors other than the size of the baby and width of the pelvic passage may enter into the determination of whether a Caesarean is necessary.

One of the things that provokes anxiety when the possibility of Caesarean is mentioned is a misconception that hangs on from the past: that if a Caesarean is done, it can be performed safely only *before* a woman goes into labor. This was true not too many years ago. For with the old type of Caesarean operation, in the years before sulfa drugs and antibiotics, infection was greatly to be feared.

If the bag of waters had been broken for more than twenty-four hours, if the woman had been in labor for any length of time, particularly if she had had any internal examinations—the obstetrician was very hesitant to perform a Caesarean, because the contents of the uterus had by that time become contaminated with bacteria. These were likely to spill into the abdominal cavity at the time the uterus was opened. Since the incision in the uterus led directly into the abdominal cavity, there would be continued leakage of infected secretions from the uterus into the abdominal cavity, resulting in the dreaded peritonitis, and death.

One of the great advances, before the antibiotic era, was an improvement in the technique of Caesarean section. The incision is now made in a part of the uterus which is under the bladder, not in direct contact with the abdominal cavity. This has become known as the "low cervical" type of Caesarean.

The combination of antibiotics and the low cervical Caesarean has rendered this operation so safe that at least one hospital has reported *no* deaths in the last *two thousand* Caesarean operations.

Today it is the exception, rather than the rule, when a first Caesarean is performed without the woman having been in labor for some time. Only in those cases where it is obvious that normal delivery is *impossible* would the decision to perform a Caesarean before labor be likely.

In *most* cases, where there is a question of the ability of the baby's head to go through his mother's pelvic passage, the disproportion is not so absolute that it may not be overcome by the strong forces of labor. The head of a baby is not made of an inflexible substance. Nature designed it in such a way that it is able to mold itself to passages that at first seemed far too narrow for it. The bones of the baby's skull are thin and parchmentlike and separated from one another, so that they can be compressed, and even overlap.

A woman is allowed to go into labor even when it appears unlikely that she will deliver normally. How long she is

allowed to remain in labor will depend on the judgment of
her obstetrician as to whether she is making satisfactory
progress. There is no longer any time limit, whether or not
the bag of waters has ruptured.

No one wishes a woman to suffer unnecessarily. As soon as
it becomes obvious that reasonable progress is not being
made, the labor may be terminated by performing a Caesarean. The Caesarean may be performed at a much earlier
stage if signs of fetal distress appear.

The Caesarean operation. The operation of Caesarean section is like any other abdominal operation. Any anesthesia
may be used that is suitable for abdominal surgery. The
choice will depend upon the preference of the individual
obstetrician. It may be influenced by special circumstances.
Very often it is performed under spinal anesthesia, since
this type of anesthesia affects only the mother and not the
baby. However, inhalation anesthesia (ether or special gases
such as cyclopropane) may also be used. In this case it is
essential that not too much time elapse from the start of the
operation until the baby is delivered, to avoid the danger of
the baby becoming too saturated with the anesthetic agent
which it receives through its mother's blood. Caesareans
have even been performed entirely under local anesthesia.

Most obstetricians perform a vertical incision, extending
in the midline from just below the navel to the pubic bone.
But for reasons of vanity, or in the excessively obese
woman, another type of incision may be performed. This incision curves downward and runs from side to side just
within the area normally covered by the pubic hair. It is ad-
vantageous in the obese since a large fold of fatty tissue
may be kept above the incision and out of the way. It is
also considered desirable for vanity's sake, because it may
leave no visible scar on the lower abdomen. Its only disadvantage is that in the event of some wound infection the
end result is apt to be more troublesome than with the more
popular vertical incision.

Only about five to ten minutes need elapse from the first
incision until the baby is delivered. Much more time is spent
in careful stitching of the uterus and overlying tissues. The
total operation is likely to consume between forty-five minutes and an hour.

Recovery after a Caesarean. Discomfort following a Caesarean is likely to be less than that encountered with most

other abdominal operations. There is no diseased organ to be removed and no necessity for handling intestines. The uterus containing the baby occupies most of the abdominal cavity—pushing the intestines out of the way. When intestines must be pushed out of the way with gauze packs, it increases the tendency to distention and gas pains.

As with normal delivery, the woman gets up out of bed early following Caesarean. Usually a firm abdominal binder is put on, the woman sits up and dangles her feet from the bed the following morning, and gets out of bed to sit in a chair that same afternoon.

This has greatly reduced the amount of discomfort from gas pains. There is some pain, naturally, in the region of the incision in the first few days, when the woman is required to get in and out of bed and walk around. By the fourth or fifth day the woman is generally walking around as freely as the woman who had a normal birth. Stitches or skin clips are usually removed on the fifth or sixth day.

The incision appears quite firmly healed at this time, although there are little crusts or scabs along the line of incision and over the points where the stitches have entered the skin. These may require two or three weeks to flake off. During this time, however, no special attention need be paid to the incision other than keeping a sterile pad of gauze over it to prevent it from rubbing against clothing as long as any raw spots remain.

In all other respects, recovery of the woman who has given birth by Caesarean is exactly the same as that of the woman who has given birth normally. The average stay in the hospital is about eight days, possibly a day longer than with normal birth. If help at home is not adequate, a few extra days in the hospital are desirable.

Pregnancies after a Caesarean. Questions always arise as soon as delivery by Caesarean is discussed: What of the future? Will it be advisable to have further pregnancies? If so, how many? And is normal delivery possible once a woman has had a Caesarean operation?

Many years ago someone coined the phrase: "Once a Caesarean, always a Caesarean." This was disputed then, and the dispute is still going on today.

There is no question that if a Caesarean operation was performed for reasons other than the size of the pelvic passages, it is possible to have a perfectly normal labor and delivery when the woman becomes pregnant again. The question about which the debate rages is: Is it *desirable* to attempt normal delivery? Is there any advantage, or does the risk of tearing the scar in the uterus outweigh the risk involved in simply performing another Caesarean at the time delivery is due?

When *either* procedure is followed with care and judgment, the risk is so small that it is quite possible that no final verdict on which is preferable will ever be reached.

It would appear far simpler, certainly (and less worrisome), to perform another Caesarean at the time the baby is due, rather than to hover anxiously over a woman in labor, wondering if the Caesarean scar in her uterus will be equal to the strain. There is no infallible sign that will warn when the scar in the uterus is likely to tear. The process of watchful waiting can only mean watchfulness—and waiting for the rupture to occur. But in a modern hospital, under careful supervision, even if the rupture does occur, it carries no grave danger to the mother. Possibly not much more than she will face with the Caesarean operation *before* labor. The baby also is likely to survive undamaged, although the risk here is somewhat increased.

There are many women who have had two, three, or more Caesarean operations. The risk in future pregnancies is so slight that no woman need hesitate to face pregnancy just because she has had a Caesarean.

There is a popular notion that some definite limit has been set to the number of Caesareans a woman may be allowed to undergo. Many doctors feel that if a woman has had three Caesarean operations she is entitled to eliminate the possibility of future pregnancy by a sterilizing operation such as the tying of the Fallopian tubes. This simply expresses their philosophy that a woman who has three children to raise has such a great obligation to them that she should not face even a minimal risk for the sake of bringing additional children into the world. Where religious convictions forbid the limitation of fertility by this method a woman may have as many children by Caesarean as she would under more normal circumstances.

Other considerations must, of course, enter into the picture—such as general health and the exact conditions found at the time each operation is performed. It is possible for repeated Caesareans eventually to cause excessive scarring of the uterus, requiring its removal. In this case, sterilization would be an incidental result of a necessary operation.

INDUCED LABOR

When is labor induced? Induction of labor means bringing on labor pains (which result in eventual delivery of the baby) *before* such pains have occurred naturally. If the pains have *already* commenced, and the cervix has begun to dilate, then any method of strengthening the pains and hastening the delivery is no longer considered induction, but *acceleration* of labor. Of course there may be some question as to whether labor is actually being induced or accelerated—depending upon the judgment of the obstetrician as to whether the woman is having true labor pains at the time or *pre*-labor contractions with some crampy sensations.

At one time it was felt that where doubt existed about the capacity of the mother's pelvis to permit passage of a full-sized baby it was wisest to induce labor early in order to have a smaller infant and an easier birth. Today, this practice has largely been abandoned—for many reasons.

First of all, the welfare of the infant precludes deliberately bringing on labor prematurely. In the second place, the weight of the baby increases much faster than the diameter of the head, which is the factor that determines whether or not the baby can pass through the mother's pelvic passages. *Very* little reduction in the diameter of the head is possible, unless the labor is brought on while the weight of the baby is far below the limit of safety.

The third reason lies in the increased safety of the operation of Caesarean section. In the old days the obstetrician had to make up his mind in advance whether a baby could be delivered normally. Once labor was allowed to go on any length of time, examinations were necessary to determine its progress. Then, especially if the water had broken, the woman had to be considered potentially infected. With each succeeding hour of labor there was a greater danger of peritonitis if a Caesarean had to be performed. But improvements in the surgical technique of Caesarean operations, plus the introduction of sulfa drugs and antibiotics, have made infection a far less fearsome complication.

Today, if there is any doubt of the mother's ability to deliver normally, the obstetrician will generally await the on-set of normal labor. Then, by observing the progress of labor, he can determine how long a trial of labor is useful. As long as there is progress, even though slow, he may feel per-fectly safe in waiting. At any time that progress ceases, and the prospect of a normal delivery appears too remote, he can terminate labor quite safely with a Caesarean operation.

In some cases labor progresses to such an extent that an attempt at delivery with instruments may be justified, even though the obstetrician is not certain that it will be success-ful. He knows how much pressure can be safely applied. If he finds that this is inadequate to effect delivery, he may de-sist from further attempts at instrument delivery and still perform a Caesarean operation with safety.

Today we do not feel that we are justified in inducing labor early—and bringing into the world a definitely premature infant—just to lessen the chance of a Caesarean.

There is room for argument over the advantages and dis-advantages of inducing labor purely as a matter of con-venience. But there is *no question* that situations do arise where it *is* desirable to induce labor—as in toxemia and post-maturity.

Methods of inducing labor. There are many techniques for the induction of labor. Probably the best known is taking castor oil. This, however, will only serve as the final spark to set off the process when the woman is actually just on the verge of spontaneous labor. In former years there were vari-ous mechanical contrivances inserted into the uterus to stim-ulate labor pains. These have largely been abandoned.

Today the most popular method of inducing labor is the injection of an extract of the pituitary gland, called pituitrin. It causes powerful contractions of the uterine muscles. If the uterus is ready, this will bring on labor.

Rupture of the bag of waters, by itself, is usually sufficient to induce labor—providing the uterus is partly open and the cervix has already thinned out.

The *combination* of injection of pituitrin and rupture of the bag of waters is almost infallible when used under proper circumstances.

When this powerful extract of the pituitary gland was first discovered many years ago, it was injected in rather large quantities, indiscriminately. The effects were so harmful that for a long time no reputable obstetrician would use it at all—before the baby was delivered—except with extreme caution. The reason for its renewed popularity in recent years has been the discovery of a new and safer method of administering this powerful drug.

Formerly it was given by injection into the muscle or under the skin. The effects were unpredictable. Sometimes a violent and sustained contraction of the uterus resulted, lasting for many minutes, threatening the life of the baby, or even causing rupture of the uterus.

The newer method is to dilute one cc. of pituitrin in one thousand cc. of water containing glucose or saline solution. This is allowed to drip very slowly into the vein, so that each drop entering the vein contains only about a twentieth part of a thousandth of a cc. of the drug. In this manner, the amount of drug in the circulation can be varied quickly. If contractions are too strong, the rate of flow can be slowed or stopped. If contractions are weak, the rate can gradually be increased. Very often the total amount injected is only about a third of a cc. of pituitrin over a period of five hours, during which time-induced labor is completed. This is only a little more than was formerly given with each injection in the muscle.

The popularity of induced labor. Any method that assures the arrival of the baby at a time convenient for everyone is bound to have a strong appeal. There is an added attraction in the possibility that sedatives may be administered before the injection of pituitrin. The woman is asleep by the time it takes effect, awakening after delivery with no recollection of any labor pains whatsoever.

The difficulty is that if the doctor promises this type of delivery "by appointment" to every patient, sooner or later he will be forced to attempt it when conditions are not quite favorable, or else go back on his word. Then he'll be faced with the choice of admitting failure and sending home a bitterly disappointed woman still bearing her baby, or else —by continuing stronger and stronger attempts at stimulation of a reluctant uterus—be tempted to exceed the safe limits of the method. The Director of Obstetrics at a New York Hospital, one of the strongest advocates of induced labor, finds that induction is possible only with about 25% of his patients. The rest go into labor spontaneously by the time conditions appear suitable for induction. Remember this the next time you hear of a doctor who delivers "all his babies by appointment."

PREMATURE BIRTH

What is premature birth? Premature birth may be defined as labor occurring before the woman is in the ninth month of pregnancy, and while the baby is under five-and-a-half pounds in weight.

The greatest cause of fetal loss today is premature birth. Practically the only way by which the number of newborn deaths can be significantly decreased is by preventing the occurrence of premature labor. Unfortunately, we know of no specific means by which premature labor can be prevented.

Statistics show that it is most common among the very young—girls in their early teens—and among the poorly nourished.

If premature birth occurs no more than eight or nine weeks before the expected date of delivery, the baby has a fairly good chance of survival. More than ten weeks before the expected date of delivery its chances are dubious. The weight of the baby is important, but its maturity is not simply a matter of pounds and ounces.

Labor and delivery. When labor occurs prematurely, it follows the same pattern as any other labor. The onset of labor pains is generally gradual, beginning with dull cramps that increase in intensity and frequency. The water may break first and there may or may not be a certain amount of bleeding.

The conduct of the labor will depend on whether the obstetrician feels that pregnancy has progressed far enough so that the baby has a reasonable chance of survival. In the interests of the infant, he will prefer to use as little as possible of pain-relieving drugs, which might tend to depress its feeble breathing mechanism, and to deliver under local anesthesia if possible.

Delivery of the small premature infant presents no problem, except in the rare case where the pelvis is *extremely* small or there is some abnormality of the position of the baby. A breech in a premature infant is common, but not a cause for concern since the baby is so small.

Care of premature babies. The great problem with premature babies is their care. They require the closest of observation, careful control of oxygen, temperature, and humidity, skillful feeding techniques (including feeding through a stomach tube), and the most expert and vigilant nursing care.

For this reason premature birth has in the past represented a financial catastrophe to the middle class. Where hospitals were not equipped with a premature nursery, special nurses were required to care for each infant twenty-four hours a day. This type of care might be necessary for weeks. Even in hospitals with premature nurseries, since three nurses are required for the care of every four to six infants, the cost is apt to be considerable, especially since so many weeks of care may be necessary before the baby is ready to go home.

Today, however, communities have taken over part of the responsibility, establishing premature centers in certain well-equipped hospitals. Babies may be transferred to these centers in portable incubators when they've been delivered in other hospitals. Here the community will take over part or even all the cost of the care until the premature infant is ready to go home.

The care of the premature baby consists, first, in the type of delivery which will cause it the least possible injury. Undue amounts of sedative drugs are avoided. Unless the baby delivers quickly and spontaneously, small forceps are used to lift the baby out without allowing too much pressure on its head. An incubator is usually warmed and ready when a premature baby is expected. The baby is immediately placed in the incubator and watched carefully. Any fluid obstructing its breathing is suctioned out. Vitamin K is immediately given to promote clotting of the blood and prevent hemorrhage. Stimulants are given if necessary.

At one time it was thought that the only concern with respect to oxygen was that its concentration be kept high enough to avoid any sign of blueness indicating insufficient oxygen. Lately it has been discovered that oxygen itself can be a poison—if the baby is allowed to remain in too high a concentration over too long a time. In recent years it was found that it was this high concentration of oxygen that caused a fibrous change behind the lens of the eye and the permanent blindness that afflicted some premature infants.

Today all premature nurseries analyze the air in the incubators regularly to avoid excessive amounts of oxygen.

How long the premature baby must remain in an incubator will depend on its degree of immaturity. Some babies, weighing only three and a half to four pounds, exhibit such vigor that within a few days no more oxygen may be required. After a period of observation it may be decided that even the incubator is no longer necessary. Just when the decision is made to take the baby out of the incubator will depend on the degree of caution exercised by the individual pediatrician or nurse.

Now that the cause of the dreaded blindness has been discovered, parents of a premature baby may face the future quite hopefully. If the baby remains vigorous after the first few days of life, with each passing day its chances of survival improve. If no warning symptoms appear, there is every reason to believe that once it reaches full-term size its chances of normal development are just as good as those of any full-term infant.

Recovery after premature delivery. Recovery of the mother after a premature delivery follows the same pattern as recovery after a full-term birth. Even though the infant was quite small, the mother need not be surprised to find that she has stitches the same as the mother of a larger infant. The obstetrician may feel it necessary to make an incision to spare the small, soft head of the baby the pressure involved in stretching the vaginal opening.

The time spent in the hospital will be about the same as that of the mother of a full-term infant. Milk formation will take place in the same way and may be suppressed in the same manner. Since premature babies are too weak to nurse, the mother who wants to breast-feed her baby later must use a breast pump. The milk obtained in this way can be fed to her baby, if possible, or fed to some other infant who needs it, until her own baby grows large enough to nurse at the breast. This is not practical in the case of a very small premature infant, which might be required to spend weeks or months in the nursery before it is ready to come home.

OTHER DELIVERY COMPLICATIONS

Breech birth. A breech delivery takes place when the position of the baby is reversed. Instead of lying in the head-down position, so that the head is born first, the baby lies in the mother's abdomen with its head up. It may be either in a squatting position or with its legs extended straight up. In either case, the breech (the buttocks) of the baby is in the lowermost position. In the squatting position, one or both feet may actually be the first part of the baby to be born.

Many women ask: "Has my baby turned yet?" This reflects the fact that many babies lie in a breech position up to the eighth month but turn to a headfirst position before delivery. This may be due to the fact that the lower part of the uterus broadens out as the end of pregnancy approaches, allowing the largest portion of the baby—the head—to be more readily accommodated.

For this reason, breech birth is much more common in premature than in full-term babies. But probably 75 per cent of infants are in the headfirst position throughout the last months of pregnancy, and do not turn at all.

Statistics indicate that the breech position carries a greater risk to the baby than the normal headfirst position. These statistics are influenced by the fact that a larger percentage of babies born in the breech position are small premature babies whose survival rate is less than full-term infants.

But even with a full-term baby, delivery in breech position is a problem to the obstetrician if there is any doubt as to the capacity of the woman's pelvis. The head of a baby is its largest and most resistant part. One can be certain, if the baby is presenting *headfirst,* that if the head delivers, the rest of the baby will follow with little difficulty. The progress of labor can be accurately estimated by the rate at which the head descends through the pelvis. If any doubt about the ability of the baby's head to deliver exists, the obstetrician may wait as long as progress appears satisfactory. When it does not, he can intervene *at any time* with a Caesarean operration. He may even go to the extent of attempting delivery with forceps. If these fail, he can still take the woman to the operating room and perform a Caesarean without harm to the mother or the baby.

With a breech, however, the situation is quite different. If it is a first baby, there is no record of performance to go by. The obstetrician makes the most careful estimate possible of the size and shape of the pelvic passages, using X-ray measurements if available. For with the breech coming first, the doctor is given no information as labor progresses which can assure him that safe delivery will be possible.

The breech of a baby is smaller in diameter than the head. Even if the mother has a narrow pelvis, labor may progress fairly rapidly, the uterus dilate, and finally the breech deliver. Not until then would the real difficulty be encountered. For the head, which was under no great pressure in the upper part of the uterus, would still be round and not shaped to the passages of the pelvis. Now the obstetrician would be faced with the task of delivering this round, unmoulded head in a matter of minutes. If he should find at this stage that the passages were too narrow, it would be too late to take the woman to the operating room for a Caesarean. He would be forced to complete the delivery, even at the risk of harming the baby.

Because of this increased risk in breech delivery, Caesarean section is performed where *any* unfavorable condition or doubt exists. In addition to the size of the baby and pelvic passages, the age of the mother and difficulty in conceiving are taken into consideration.

In women who have previously delivered average-sized babies with no difficulty, the occurrence of a breech should not be a cause for concern.

Multiple births. By far the most common type of multiple birth is twins, which occur once in every 85 deliveries. Twins do not usually give rise to any difficulty in birth. One reason is that each of the twins tends to be smaller than an average baby, and thus delivers more easily. The second reason is that with twins there is a greater likelihood of premature birth, making each of the twins smaller yet. Caesarean operations because of narrow pelvic passages are less often necessary in twin pregnancies.

Labor takes place exactly as it does in normal birth. The most common position for the babies is for both to present their heads first. The next most common position is for the first-born twin to be headfirst, the second in breech position. Delivery of the first twin proceeds exactly the same as delivery of a single baby. Each twin lies within its own bag of waters, whether they are identical twins or fraternal twins.

One reads in the newspaper from time to time accounts of a second twin born hours or even days following the delivery of the first twin. It is not the usual practice to allow such a delay. Once the first twin is born, there is a certain risk involved in waiting too long for normal delivery of the second twin. The placenta may separate as the uterus contracts to a smaller size following delivery of the first twin. When the placenta separates, the oxygen supply to the second twin is cut off. It would die unless delivered in a very short time. For this reason the obstetrician prefers not to wait.

If the second twin is presenting as a breech, the doctor may simply rupture the bag of waters, grasp the feet, and extract the second twin as a breech delivery. If the second twin is presenting headfirst, the doctor has a choice of procedures: he may rupture the bag of waters and allow the mother to bear down for a normal second birth; he may be able to press the head of the second twin far enough down into the pelvis to be able to apply forceps and deliver. Or he may find it simpler, if the head is still high, to turn the second twin around in an operation known as "internal podalic version." He pushes up the head and pulls down the feet, so that on rupturing the bag of waters he can deliver the baby as a breech.

The case of twins joined together, the so-called Siamese twins, is so extremely rare that no woman need give it a thought.

Bleeding before delivery as cause for Caesarean. In the final months of pregnancy, vaginal bleeding may occur for a variety of reasons. The harmless type of bleeding is staining —the mixture of mucus and blood that occurs as labor is about to begin. But if there is a sudden gush of blood, unaccompanied by pain, there is a serious possibility that a condition known as "placenta previa" exists.

In this condition the placenta has planted itself in the lowermost portion of the uterus. Part of it is very close to— or actually covers—the cervix, the portion of the uterus that must open as labor begins. In such a situation, even before actual labor has occurred, the stretching of the lower portion of the uterus causes portions of the placenta to separate. Bleeding results.

Treatment of this condition will depend on a variety of factors. In a first pregnancy, particularly where the woman is close enough to the expected date of labor—where the baby seems large enough to survive—Caesarean section is the preferred type of treatment. By this means a living baby is practically assured, and the placenta is removed before there is opportunity for excessive loss of blood.

But in some cases this bleeding may occur in the seventh month or even earlier. In these cases the obstetrician will be hesitant to perform a Caesarean because the baby is too small to survive. He will attempt various measures to control bleeding, making sure there is blood available for replacement. If bleeding is not too excessive, the woman may be kept in the hospital under close observation for a long time, in the hope that further episodes of bleeding will not be too serious. The pregnancy can go on for several weeks more, until a living baby can be secured.

If the hemorrhage is too severe to permit waiting, the doctor must perform an immediate Caesarean. If the woman has borne previous children, and the cervix is partly dilated, it may be possible to induce labor and effect normal delivery. After the water is broken and the firm contractions of the uterus force the baby's head down, it may serve as a pressure bandage to check bleeding while labor progresses.

Another form of bleeding, occurring before or during labor, is due to separation of a placenta that has implanted *normally* —in the upper portion of the uterus. This type of separation is usually painful. The woman may first notice a dull, constant pain—associated with a hardening of her entire uterus —before any external bleeding occurs. Usually it is only after this pain has persisted for some time that a trickle of blood or passage of clots will be noted.

These cases tend to be more dangerous than those in which the placenta has abnormally implanted low in the uterus. In this case the hemorrhage is concealed. A woman may lose sufficient blood to cause shock due to bleeding which is entirely confined within her uterus—none having as yet escaped through the vagina to become visible.

This condition is also more dangerous for the baby, who receives oxygen through the placenta. If enough of the placenta separates, the baby must be lost. Where the condition is serious enough, a Caesarean must be performed in the interests of the mother, even though it is known that the baby is no longer living. In less serious cases there is only a partial separation, at the edge of the placenta, and most of the bleeding is external. Under these circumstances the obstetrician must decide whether normal delivery is likely to occur soon enough so that the life of the mother and baby will not be jeopardized. If bleeding is extensive, even though the woman has had other babies quickly, it may be safer to perform a Caesarean operation.

"Dry birth." There is no such thing as "dry birth." There is a notion that if the bag of waters breaks sometime before the onset of labor pains all this fluid will drain away and a difficult labor and delivery will follow. To this notion the term "dry birth" has been applied.

The basis for this belief lies in the fact that where the baby's head cannot "drop" into the pelvis—either because the pelvis is relatively small or because the baby is in some abnormal position—a large sac of fluid lies at the lowest portion of the uterus and is compressed against the opening in the uterus (the cervix). The pressure created by the moderately strong contractions before labor is likely to cause it to rupture, with the escape of a large amount of fluid.

Because there is then no portion of the baby pressing against the cervix to help it to dilate, labor may be slow in following. And when it does occur, it is likely to be long and difficult. But this is not because of the dryness due to lack of fluid. It is because of the abnormal position or the narrow pelvis that caused this premature rupture of the bag of waters in the first place.

When other conditions are favorable—when the cervix is thin and partly dilated, the baby's head low in the pelvis—labor that is induced by breaking the water is likely to be even more rapid than spontaneous labor with the bag of waters intact.

The term dry birth is a misnomer. Whatever difficulties may follow rupture of the bag of waters, they have nothing to do with the dryness due to the loss of fluid.

"Born with a caul." In practically all births, the point of rupture of the bag of waters enlarges during labor so that the baby's head passes through the opening in the bag of waters before it is born. But in some instances either the leak is high—above the baby's face—or else the bag of waters does not rupture at all. The baby is born with a transparent layer of membrane covering its face. This is known as being "born with a caul."

It has no scientific significance. Naturally this membrane must be opened and peeled away before the baby can breathe.

At one time there was a superstitious belief that infants born with the membrane covering their face were gifted with power to foresee the future.

CHAPTER 15

Your New Baby

In the delivery room. At the time of delivery your baby is placed across your abdomen; mucus and fluid are removed from its throat so that is breathing passages will not be obstructed. The cord is clamped, cut, and finally tied. Then your baby is placed in a heated crib in the delivery room.

The hospital makes certain that you get your own baby. You need have no fear about this. The few claims that mistakes have been made have been so widely publicized as to make one think it is a frequent occurrence. It practically never happens.

The technique of making sure your baby is properly identified varies in different institutions. One typical method is to make two bracelets with your name spelled out in beads. One of these bracelets is placed on your wrist as soon as you enter the labor room. The other is attached to it. When you give birth, this second bracelet, identical with the one sealed on your wrist, is sealed around the wrist of the baby. As an additional safeguard, a certificate on specially prepared paper is in the delivery room. On this certificate the baby's footprints are recorded, as well as your thumbprints. Your name is inscribed upon this sheet, which is placed in the infant's chart. The baby is never taken from the delivery room without first comparing the name on its wrist with the name on your wrist.

If you have not been deeply sedated, you will probably be awake enough in the delivery room to be shown your baby. Naturally, your recollection of this will not always be the clearest. You should realize that the baby may be difficult to recognize at this stage. Its hair is wet and matted with secretions. Frequently there are stains of the baby's stool. There is a white cheesy material on the skin known as vernix, which clings and is difficult to wipe away. And the baby may be stained with some clotted blood from your vagina. All this gives your baby an appearance that is somewhat alarming.

Most delivery rooms do not have scales, and the obstetrician can only guess the weight of your baby at this time. The baby is not weighed until it is taken to the nursery, which may not be until you leave the delivery room.

In the nursery. In the nursery your baby is given a bath to remove the secretions and the vernix on its skin. It is likely to be twenty minutes to a half hour before it is ready for presentation to its father.

At this time your baby may be placid and sleeping, or it may be crying lustily. Its eyes may be wide open or firmly shut. It can see, as far as reacting to light or darkness, from the moment of birth. But it is unable to focus its eyes, and cannot recognize or consciously follow objects. It has no perception of depth, distance, or size—or any of the other attributes which an adult would consider vision. But for those who have set off flash bulbs to record this moment, the reaction of the baby to this sudden flash of light has been unmistakable. (Incidentally, this flash of light is absolutely harmless as far as the baby's eyes are concerned.)

Feeding the baby. During the first twenty-four hours of life babies frequently spit up considerable amounts of mucus. Some of this has been swallowed in the course of delivery; some is the result, possibly, of irritation of the nasal passages with secretions that have been inhaled in the uterus and birth canal.

Nature has made no provision for a child to obtain any real nourishment during the first three days of life—before the mother's milk supply becomes established. It is not necessary to press artificial feedings too early in life. Usually the baby will not suck too effectively at this time. Furthermore, while it is engaged in bringing up mucus, the addition of formula simply increases the danger of plugging its air passages.

The usual routine is to give nothing at all to the baby in the first twelve hours of life. During the next twelve hours it may be offered water—with or without a certain amount of milk-sugar added. It is only after twenty-four hours that it is started on a very dilute formula. It is not expected to take any great quantities of this.

The baby's weight. Babies lose weight in the first few days of life. No matter how many times mothers are told that this is perfectly normal, few can resist a feeling of anxiety as they wait for their babies to stop losing weight and start gaining.

The reason for the baby's weight loss is not starvation. The baby loses weight after delivery for the same reason that *you* lose weight after delivery, even though you are eating adequate amounts of food. During pregnancy, your internal secretions cause your body to store up increased amounts of salt and fluid in the tissues. These are lost rapidly following delivery. You give birth to a child weighing about seven pounds, a placenta weighing about a pound, and a pound or two of water—for a total of no more than ten pounds. Yet you will find during the course of the first week in the hospital that you have lost eighteen or twenty pounds. This extra eight to ten pounds represents loss of body fluid.

The baby's tissues are also supersaturated with fluid, because its body also received the effects of your hormones. Therefore, in the first few days of life, your baby, too, must lose this excess fluid from its tissues.

Seeing the baby. If you were not conscious enough to recall seeing your baby in the delivery room, it will be brought for your inspection as soon as the medication you were given has worn off.

How often the baby is brought to you for feeding depends on the routine of the hospital. In some hospitals, mothers give their babies the 10, 2, 6, and 10 P.M. feedings as soon as the baby is on regular feedings. Other hospitals feel that it is more important for the mothers to have rest than to practice feeding, and may give the mother the baby to feed only once a day (and not until the fourth day after delivery). In the meantime, the baby will be brought for a visit once a day.

Of course, as soon as you feel strong enough, you can accompany visitors to the nursery when the babies are being shown. Each hospital has a routine as far as showing the babies to visitors is concerned. In hospitals with visiting hours twice a day there is usually a half hour in each visiting time for the showing of babies. The babies are simply brought to a window through which visitors can view them.

Obviously, it would interfere too much with the work of the nursery nurses if the babies were to be shown every time a visitor requested it.

Circumcision. The practice of circumcision has become quite widespread in this country. It is no longer regarded simply as a religious rite. The operation consists of removing the loose fold of skin that normally covers the end of the penis when it is not in erection. The arguments for this operation are primarily hygienic. It makes for greater cleanliness. Normal infants frequently are born with a tight and adherent foreskin that cannot be pulled back to expose the end of the penis. Beneath it certain secretions tend to accumulate. Occasionally infection can set in, causing a painful inflammation.

It is frequently not possible at birth to be sure which babies may have such troubles later on. If one waits, a fair percentage of foreskins that are difficult to retract at birth may be normally retractable later. But the operation of circumcision becomes much more troublesome with each passing week.

On the newborn infant no anesthesia is required. The incision is quick, the pain fleeting. The infant does not seem to be made uncomfortable once the operation has been completed, even though the operative area may appear rather raw and somewhat swollen for a few days. But an infant a month or two old is much more aware of bodily sensations. He will need anesthesia, which requires that all feedings be withheld for at least eight hours. This, in itself, is a formidable undertaking.

The religious ritual of circumcision must be performed on the eighth day following birth. It may be deferred if the condition of the child is not satisfactory at this time, but it cannot be done earlier for any reason.

As a medical procedure, however, circumcision may be undertaken at any time during the normal week's stay in the hospital. It is customary not to perform the operation if the baby is bordering on premature size.

The "soft spot." Your infant's head is composed of thin, flat bones, which are not joined together. They are separated by spaces known as "suture lines." The forehead is formed by two frontal bones; the sides of the head, by the two parietal bones; the back of the head, by the V-shaped occipital bone. Where the occipital bone joins the two parietal bones in a

Y there is a small opening known as the small, or posterior fontanelle. Where the two parietal bones and the frontal bones meet—at the top of the head—is the large fontanelle, known as the "soft spot." This large fontanelle is not completely closed until the baby is twelve to eighteen months old.

There is no truth to the notion that one must be particularly cautious in touching the soft spot. When the obstetrician is trying to determine the position of the baby's head inside the mother, he is guided by pressing firmly against either one of these openings. Skin is too tough to puncture with the finger. You need not be afraid of any dire consequences as a result of touching the brain through it.

CHAPTER 16

Getting Back to Normal

Return to your room. Exactly how long you will remain in the delivery room after giving birth depends on a variety of circumstances. Ideally, it should depend entirely on the circumstances of your delivery—whether it was difficult; whether you were in labor a long time; whether there was an unusually large amount of blood lost at the time of delivery; whether your uterus displayed a tendency to relax, causing further oozing of blood.

These *are* the main considerations. But other practical necessities have to be taken into account. The number of delivery rooms in any hospital is limited. If other women are ready to deliver, you will have to be moved back to your room sooner. Close observation must now be continued in your own room, rather than in the delivery room.

The effect of medication you received in labor and delivery is a factor in determing how soon it is advisable to return you to your own room. One of the criteria by which delivery-room nurses and the doctor will judge this is how soon you are fully aware of your surroundings, so that if you need anything you will know how to call for assistance, instead of trying to get out of bed in a semi-conscious state.

How long it takes to become fully aware of your surroundings and react normally depends on the type of anesthetic or medication employed. The woman who has had natural childbirth, or a local anesthetic with only a moderate amount of medication, will be wide awake almost as soon as the delivery is over. The woman who has been very heavily sedated by a doctor who believes in the utmost in painlessness may not be aware of what has occurred for many hours after delivery.

General anesthesia (ether, gas, or any other form of inhalation anesthetic) will continue its effects for a time that depends on the depth of anesthesia that was necessary. This, in turn, depends on the difficulty of delivery, the length of time needed to repair the incision, and so forth.

Spinal anesthesia, or saddle block, may leave a woman numb—more or less paralyzed—from the waist down for a matter of an hour or two. But she will be fully conscious, unless she has received medication in addition.

When you are returned to your own room you will be put to bed and made comfortable. Then your husband and other close relatives will be allowed to see you. It is not necessarily desirable that your husband just say a few words and quickly leave. If you are still slightly under the influence of medication, the doctor may prefer that someone remain in the room with you to make sure a nurse is called when necessary. Of course, if you have been given a sedative to relieve discomfort, it will be less effective if you are disturbed by talking.

Getting out of bed. Getting back to normal begins when you get out of bed and take a few steps. The attitude toward getting out of bed has undergone a tremendous change. Before World War II many of the most eminent obstetricians were accustomed to keeping new mothers strictly in bed for at least a week following delivery. In many hospitals ten days was considered the minimum for absolute bed rest before women were allowed to set foot on the floor. Ten, twelve, or even fourteen days was considered the optimum duration of the hospital stay.

The reasoning behind this practice was that after delivery the muscles that support the uterus are stretched and weakened, and the uterus itself is still large and heavy. It seemed logical to assume that, after giving birth, if the heavy uterus was caused to sag by the force of gravity when a woman stood up, it would contribute to the "dropping" of the womb that affects many middle-aged women.

A minority of obstetricians, even at that time, advocated what is known as "early ambulation"—getting the new mother out of bed as soon as possible. They felt there were two benefits. First of all, the longer *anyone* remains in bed, the weaker he feels when he does get up. Even a perfectly healthy person, if forced to remain in bed for several days, will feel pins and needles in his feet on first getting out of bed and might feel weak and faint. Therefore, these doctors advocated that women be allowed to get out of bed as early as the second day following birth—to exercise their muscles.

The other argument for early ambulation was that walking around at an earlier stage promoted the circulation of blood in the dilated veins of the lower extremities and pelvis, making development of the dread complication of blood clots less likely.

However, before the war these few doctors were obeyed by their patients only in fear and trepidation. Some didn't dare to tell their mothers that they had already been out of bed as early as the third day after delivery.

It was not science, but practical necessity, that swung the pendulum so far in the direction of early ambulation. During the war hospital space became limited, and the maternity services crowded. Women couldn't remain so long if everybody was to have the privilege of delivering in the hospital. When it was necessary to send a woman home in four or five days, it became necessary to allow her to walk about earlier so that she would feel strong enough to go home at that time.

With the shortage of nurses, it was also imperative that women be able to help themselves, to go to the bathroom instead of using a bedpan. Doctors were forced to try letting women out of bed earlier. When no dire results were observed, this practice became more and more popular. Today it is practically unheard of for a new mother to remain in bed more than twenty-four hours, even after a Caesarean.

How much this has reduced blood clots in the veins it is difficult to say. There is still no reliable basis for comparison. Whether it will increase the disability due to dropped wombs only time will tell. The evidence so far indicates that it will not.

The chief advantages of this early ambulation are that you feel stronger more quickly, are able to control your functions better, empty your bladder more easily.

There is only one evident disadvantage in getting up, walking, and sitting so early. It has probably increased the amount of discomfort from stitches over what women used to feel when they lay quietly in bed for the first five or six days.

Most doctors discourage too much activity immediately after you have your baby. Getting out of bed two or three times a day just to go the the bathroom, perhaps walking about in your own room a bit, is sufficient exercise for the first day or two. After that, you should allow yourself to be up for longer and longer periods—not overtiring yourself or exceeding your strength.

Urinating. The usual routine now is to allow the mother to get out of bed the day following delivery to go to the bathroom. You will be expected to empty your bladder within about twelve hours after giving birth. There is no fixed rule about this. If you were under considerable amount of anesthesia, had a long labor, have not been drinking much water, and there is no reason to believe that your bladder is distended, you will simply be encouraged to drink freely and given further opportunities to void. If, however, the nurse finds that the bladder is distended, and you are unable to void, she may catheterize you.

This is not an uncomfortable procedure. Nor should it alarm you. The irritation that the tissues have suffered in the stretching of childbirth, plus the incision, causes a spasm of the muscles that close the neck of the bladder. You may find it difficult to relax these muscles in order to empty the bladder. It occurs frequently, particularly among the high-strung. If it does happen, your bladder is emptied by inserting a soft rubber tube (or catheter).

How often this is done depends upon how distended the bladder becomes. Normally, if the bladder contains more than a quart of urine, you will become quite uncomfortable. And since you are drinking more than usual in an effort to urinate normally, the bladder will fill up quite quickly.

Sometimes a woman thinks she is doing well because she manages to void fairly frequently. But this may be an overflow voiding, in which she keeps almost a quart of urine in the bladder and simply empties the excess. In spite of frequent urinating, she might be aware of increasing lower abdominal pains, the cause of which is soon apparent when she is catheterized and as much as two quarts of urine removed.

Every woman will eventually urinate normally and without difficulty. So do not become worried even if this catheterization procedure has to be carried out quite frequently. And in at least 90 per cent of the cases it will not be necessary at all.

Bowel movement. Bowel movement usually does not occur spontaneously following the birth of a baby. For some reason, even after the most normal birth, without any stitches, the intestinal tract seems simply to relax and go on vacation. Although you may eat normally, it would be unusual for your bowels to move before the third day. Usually the second night after delivery a cathartic is given. If this is effective, nothing more need be done.

The choice of cathartic is an individual matter. What is mild for one woman may be drastic for another. Your doctor will take this into consideration.

Another factor that is taken into consideration is whether or not you are nursing your baby. If you *are* nursing your baby, some form of cathartic must be given which is not absorbed, because some laxatives are actually excreted in the milk and may have a cathartic action on the baby.

If, in spite of the cathartic on the second night, there is no movement on the third day, your doctor may feel that an enema to clear the lower bowel will make you more comfortable.

Many women are extremely apprehensive about the first bowel movement. As was explained in the section on incisions, the incision to lengthen the vagina for delivery must extend from the lower end of the vagina close to the rectum —either directly in the midline or to one side. The sensation of tenderness which you experience will be felt in the region of the rectum. Therefore, you may be afraid that moving your bowels is going to be extremely painful. Actually, this is not the case. There is no greater discomfort in moving the bowels than in urinating following delivery. The position itself may be somewhat uncomfortable, but the actual passage of stool will cause no pain.

Diet. Immediately after delivery you will desire very little food, especially if you have had medication or anesthesia. But the following day a perfectly normal diet may be taken.

"Afterpains." After delivery of a first baby there are usually few cramps experienced that are strong enough to disturb the mother. The uterus appears to contract firmly once the baby is delivered, and remains firmly contracted.

But with *subsequent* babies, the uterus has a tendency to relax slightly and then contract again strongly. Each time this happens you will experience a cramp not unlike a labor pain. These cramps are generally felt exactly in the location where you felt your labor pains or menstrual pains.

If you are nursing, you will find that the stimulation of your breasts will stimulate these contractions, causing increased intensity of these "afterpains." Preparations of ergot, which you may be given to prevent excessive bleeding by stimulating contractions of the uterus, will also tend to increase the severity of afterpains. Many a woman has been disappointed when she was given a small white pill—feeling that it was a sedative that would make her feel more comfortable—and severe cramps followed instead.

Afterpains are generally most intense during the first two days, then they gradually diminish.

Bleeding after delivery. The average amount of blood lost in a normal birth at the time of delivery is from one quarter of a pint to a pint. Probably a large percentage of women lose well *over* a pint without feeling weak or any other ill effects. Nature has provided the pregnant woman with an expanded volume of somewhat-diluted blood. Even though you lose as much as a pint of blood, within a day or two your blood count will be as high (or even higher) than it was before delivery. The blood becomes more concentrated as excess fluid is eliminated from your blood stream and tissues.

On the day of delivery small gushes of blood and clots are not unusual. This flow of bright red blood continues in a moderate amount, perhaps somewhat heavier than at the height of a menstrual period, during the first few days. After about three days the discharge becomes less bloody. It tends to have a thick, pinkish character that gradually becomes lighter in color. Finally, by the eighth to the tenth day it becomes almost a whitish to a salmon-pink in color, changing to brownish at times. This type of discharge will probably persist for some three to four weeks following birth.

The excitement of leaving the hospital, or of the first days at home, often causes a recurrence of heavy red bleeding.

Stitches. Women frequently approach delivery with an excessive fear of stitches, because of the gossip to which they have been exposed. You may have gathered the impression that the pain is very severe and may persist long enough to threaten your future sex life. Actually, with today's practice of getting out of bed and sitting early after delivery, it is inevitable that an incision in the part of the body on which one sits would cause some discomfort.

There is usually a burning sensation toward the rectum in the first few hours after delivery. Then it subsides, so that you are scarcely aware of it until you make a sudden movement contracting the muscles around the incision. A cough or sneeze will definitely bring it to your attention. And when you get out of bed to go to the bathroom, or sit in a chair, you must expect the discomfort of putting pressure on a recent incision.

This is never incapacitating, however. Sedative pills, such as codeine, are sufficient to relieve any discomfort. Anesthetic ointments or sprays can soothe only the surface, and do not reach the deeper tissues where much of the pain originates. But they are useful to relieve chafing and irritation of sanitary pads. Application of heat is frequently helpful. Your doctor may order a heating lamp once or twice a day for several days, to reduce swelling and promote healing.

The stitches most frequently used are made of catgut, and need not be removed. They simply dissolve. However, this catgut may take more than two weeks to dissolve, while the incision itself is usually healed by the fifth day. Therefore, if pain persists or grows worse at this time because swelling of tissue has made the stitches taut, your doctor may decide to relieve it by simply cutting the stitches. This is not at all painful.

How long a sense of discomfort will persist varies greatly. Some women may have very little discomfort in the hospital, and be practically free of it by the time they go home. Other women, even though their incisions heal as well, may continue to experience pain for a longer time—not anything very sharp, but a dull, drawing ache. This does not indicate that anything is wrong. Hot baths are helpful, but are not advisable for two or three weeks after delivery.

A *few* women may notice a sensitive feeling in the region of the scar even months after delivery—particularly in the engorged state preceding a menstrual period. This does not cause any disability, and eventually subsides.

Post-pregnancy depression. During the stay in the hospital —usually around the fourth or fifth day—a certain percentage of mothers will experience a feeling of depression, popularly known as "maternity blues." For reasons they cannot explain they find tears very near the surface. One thoughtless word from the husband or a visitor, a minor problem about announcements or baby furniture, is sufficient to release a torrent.

These mothers are unable to explain their reaction, and are quite upset by it. All they know is that they feel terrible, and the world appears a very dreary place.

This type of emotional reaction has nothing to do with how much the baby was wanted. Women who have ardently desired an infant for years are just as likely to suffer from such a depression as the mother for whom pregnancy was a sheer accident.

Fortunately, most women recover rapidly, and need only some mildly stimulating drugs for a few days to help relieve the symptoms. No case need cause great concern, unless there is a history of serious emotional disturbance previous to the pregnancy.

The cause for this feeling of depression is physical rather than psychological. The system of the mother has been flooded with hormones during pregnancy. These are rapidly eliminated following birth. This sudden drop in hormone level is responsible for the change in mood. The same effect is noted in men as well as women when hormone treatments are suddenly stopped after they have been given for a long time.

If you nurse your baby. If you are nursing your baby, you will probably be encouraged to drink milk, and will be cautioned about certain foods. Some feel that excessive amounts of fruit or chocolate affect the quality of milk, and thus the baby. There is no scientific proof that this is so. But certainly it is sensible to make sure that your diet is well balanced and relatively plain.

In planning to nurse your baby, you will have taken preliminary care during the last weeks of pregnancy to soften your nipples and stimulate their erectile powers. It is difficult, in the abstract, to teach the art of nursing. You will require the guidance of a nurse, who will show you how to give your baby the breast, how to keep it awake and interested, how to make sure its nose is not obstructed by the breast so that it can breathe freely and be able to suck.

The breasts are carefully washed and kept covered by little sterile squares of gauze. Some bland ointment is generally used—such as vitamin A and D ointment—to promote a healthy skin that will resist cracking. If cracking occurs, the obstetrician's advice will have to be sought. He will tell you what ointment to apply, whether a shield should be used, or—if the cracking is severe—whether the attempt at nursing should be given up altogether.

The general rule for nursing is to apply the baby to the breast for the first time about twenty-four hours after birth. If you gave birth in the middle of the night, the first time will be the early-morning feeding the second day after delivery.

The routine most popular today is to allow the baby to nurse on both breasts at each feeding. In general it is considered advisable not to allow the baby to suck for too long, or to attempt to nurse too frequently, before the milk supply is established. This is generally about the third day. Up to this time the baby obtains only a small amount of a pre-milk secretion known as colostrum. This is said to provide valuable immune substances. It has some laxative effect. But its exact importance has not been proved.

Until there is a real supply of milk, it is adequate stimulation for the breasts if the baby is nursed only twice a day. Once the milk supply is established, it is customary to feed the baby every four hours. During the stay in the hospital you should be allowed to have nights of uninterrupted sleep if possible. A bottle is given in place of the 2 A.M. feeding, unless you have so much milk that it is uncomfortable for you to go eight hours without nursing. In such cases you would have to give all six feedings.

If you do not nurse. There is little if any evidence that liquids—taken in normal quantities—will increase the amount of breast engorgement. The drinking of milk will have no more effect on engorgement of breasts than the drinking of an equal quantity of water. The breasts do not make milk out of milk any more than out of other foods.

Advice is given from all quarters as to what women should do to avoid "caking of the breasts" if they are not nursing. In the old days, before hormones were used, it was the custom to try to make a woman as dry as possible. A saline cathartic was given to produce liquid stools that further dehydrated her. Her breasts were tightly bound. Possibly she noted less discomfort in the breasts themselves, because of general misery induced by these measures.

Since about 1940 it has been known that hormones may be used to suppress the formation of milk by the breasts. Originally such hormones could be given only by injection, and were quite expensive. Therefore, before the war this method was not too popular. Male sex hormone was injected in large amounts for two or three days, and frequently reduced the amount of engorgement of the breasts.

Then a synthetic hormone that could be taken by mouth—called stilbesterol—was introduced. At first this was given in rather large doses—as much as fifteen to thirty milligrams a day for four days. With this dosage the woman noticed no engorgement of the breasts when it usually appears—on the third or fourth day. But in many cases there was a distinct rebound several days later. The breasts became just as engorged and painful as they would have without the hormone. The only difference was that the effect was delayed.

Since then it has been found that much smaller doses are equally effective, and if tapered off gradually there is much less tendency to this delayed engorgement.

Many hormone preparations other than stilbesterol are in use today. There is very little difference in their effects. They all work on the same principle.

The high level of female hormone in your blood stream before delivery has an inhibiting effect on the pituitary gland. When you give birth, the production of these hormones falls off sharply, and they are rapidly eliminated from your blood stream. This sudden dropping of the level of the hormones in the blood stream causes a release of pituitary secretion—a substance known as prolactin—that stimulates the breasts. The veins of the breasts become engorged with blood, swollen and hard, and then the breasts begin the manufacture of milk.

(It is interesting to note that the baby also has its blood stream saturated with the mother's female sex hormone while in the uterus. After being born, the source of the hormone is removed, and the hormone in its blood stream is rapidly eliminated. The baby's own pituitary gland is thereby stimulated—and for this reason the baby's breasts often become engorged, secreting what has been known in the past as "Witch's Milk." This same stimulation of the pituitary gland by elimination of the mother's hormones may also cause a menstruation in female infants at about five to seven days of life.)

Hormones may or may not be used to suppress lactation (production of milk) if you do not desire to nurse your baby. If they are used in moderate amount, your breasts may become slightly hard and tender for a day or so in spite of their administration. This is actually rather desirable. By the time you go home from the hospital your breasts will be soft and comfortable, and no further discomfort is to be anticipated. If there is to be any engorgement it is preferable that it occur in the hospital, where sedatives and the assistance of a nurse are readily available.

As far as secretion is concerned, a certain amount of leakage from the breasts will almost invariably take place whether or not hormones are given to suppress engorgement. This may occur in the hospital, or shortly after going home. No treatment is ever necessary for this. It will disappear spontaneously, though it may continue for several days or weeks. In some cases it recurs in small amounts at the time of your menstrual period even months later. Nothing more is required than absorbent material within your brassière to protect your clothing.

Occasionally, when your breasts become swollen, you may also note a painful swelling under one or both arms. This may alarm you, because you know that glands in that area become swollen when there is infection draining into them. But this is not the case at this time. Such swellings are due to the presence of displaced breast tissue in the armpits. This tissue cannot be felt until it becomes engorged along with your breasts. It will disappear completely when the engorgement subsides.

Going home. The average stay in the hospital is now about seven days. In some hospitals, however, it is still the custom to remain only about five days—as it was during the crowded days of the war.

When you go home, you will still be staining. Occasionally the excitement of leaving may bring on a heavier flow of blood, even an alarming gush. Medication may be required to stimulate firmer contractions of the uterus, and bed rest for a time is advisable.

It is not unusual for stitches to be slightly tender at this time, although no special care is normally required.

Activity during your first weeks at home. When you go home, it is important that you increase your activities *gradually*. Although you have been discharged from the hospital, you are by no means completely restored to normal. It is probably best for you to remain in the house for another week, for once you allow yourself to go outdoors, to shop or visit, it will be difficult for you to exercise proper restraint.

You should, if possible, be off your feet part of the morning, rest during the afternoon, retire early at night.

Visiting should be restricted to only the closest friends and relatives during the first week.

While you were in the hospital, you were given special care after elimination. You used sterile cotton and soap for cleansing purposes, rather than toilet tissue. It is wisest to continue this type of care at home if there is any feeling of rawness persisting in the region of the stitches.

The climbing of stairs is in many instances a necessity. It does not constitute any grave menace, even if you have had a Caesarean operation. But such exertions should be kept to a minimum. Arrangements should be made so that you do not have to ascend and descend stairs more than once or twice a day.

During the second week you will go outside, increasing your activities from day to day. By the time your baby is about three weeks old you can be on a fairly normal schedule.

Still prohibited are douching and sexual intercourse. The advisability of tub bathing at this time is still debated. But by the end of the fourth week, when staining is minimal, there is no serious objection to tub bathing if you prefer it. Showers, of course, have been taken since the early days in the hospital.

How soon the baby can be taken out should be discussed with your pediatrician or family doctor. His decision will be influenced by climate more than any other factor.

Getting back your figure. If you gained no more than twenty to twenty-five pounds during the nine months of pregnancy, you will have little trouble regaining your normal weight. When you leave the hospital you should be no more than four or five pounds above the weight at which you started pregnancy. These four or five pounds should represent no serious problem to a woman of average will power, and may even drop off spontaneously.

The woman who has gained *excessively* during pregnancy (where it has not simply been due to fluid retention) is faced with a problem. Weight gains of forty to fifty pounds are not unheard of if a woman has indulged herself without limit. Such women will have to diet strenuously to regain their figures. There is no reason why the dieting should not commence on the day of delivery. It should have commenced much earlier than that.

The diet followed in such a case may be just as rigid as the diet followed by any woman who had not been pregnant. Naturally, this diet must allow—as it must at any phase of life—sufficient bulk to promote elimination, sufficient protein to replace that lost in the wear and tear on the body, and adequate vitamins and minerals.

The question of dieting for the woman who is nursing a baby presents a little more difficult problem, since she must eat enough to provide rich milk for her baby. But actually it should be easier for her to lose weight, since she is losing many calories in the form of milk. If she has large fat deposits, there is no reason why—if she is taking a diet adequate in minerals, protein, and vitamins—she cannot utilize her excess stores of fat to provide the cream for the milk.

Most women will be dissatisfied with the flabbiness of their abdominal muscles following delivery. Nature must allow these muscles to stretch in order to accommodate a full-term baby within the abdomen. You should not expect them to snap back like rubber bands the minute the baby is delivered. This requires weeks, and if these muscles have stretched excessively due to fluid accumulation or a very large baby (or twins), they may never *completely* return to their prepregnancy condition.

At one time it was popular to bind the mother's abdomen as soon as the baby was born, in the belief that this hastened the restoration of muscle tone and would improve the figure. Few obstetricians believe in its value today. There is no harm in wearing some form of support—either a hospital binder or a girdle, since the sagging of these muscles may make some mothers appear still pregnant when they stand. However, recovery of your figure cannot depend on the use of external support.

It would appear unwise to place these overstretched muscles under tension immediately by attempting to perform abdominal exercises. Your muscles should be allowed a minimum of three weeks to take up some of the slack and regain their tone before further strengthening by exercise is attempted.

Recovery of your figure will reflect, largely, the degree of muscular development that you attained *before* pregnancy. Pregnancy itself should not cause specific defects in your figure that require special exercises to overcome. All the exercises that are prescribed for improving the figure and posture of a woman who has just had a baby would be equally effective for the woman who had never been pregnant.

The chief purpose of all such exercises is to strengthen the muscles of the abdominal wall and back, which receive too

FIGURE E.

Post-Pregnancy Exercises to Tighten Your Abdominal Muscles

1. Lie flat on your back. Raise your body till it is supported only by the backs of your shoulders and the soles of your feet.
2. Lie flat on your back. Raise one leg without bending at the knee, then lower, and raise other leg.
3. Lie flat on your back, arms folded across your chest. Raise and lower your body without bending your knees.

little use in a civilization that rarely calls for climbing or carrying of heavy burdens. Calisthenics are the price of comfortable living. Typical exercises for improving the figure are illustrated above.

First checkup examination. There is some difference of opinion among obstetricians as to how soon a checkup examination is advisable. The most popular interval is about six weeks. By this time a fairly large percentage of women will have returned to normal as far as the size of the uterus is concerned. Staining will have ceased.

FIGURE F. Knee-Chest Position

This is used to induce a "tipped" uterus to come forward into normal position.

However, there is an impression among many women that they should wait until they have had a menstrual period before going for their examination. How soon this first menstrual period will appear is unpredictable. Bleeding of any amount in less than five weeks must be regarded with suspicion, rather than as a normal period. Usually six weeks is the minimum interval for a menstrual period to occur following a full-term birth. But it is not at all unusual for the period to be delayed for ten or twelve weeks—and even longer if you are nursing your baby.

Therefore, it is impractical to let the appearance of a menstrual period determine the time for your examination.

During the first examination, the doctor will normally weigh you to see how well you have returned to you former weight, check your blood pressure and urine. He may take a blood count to see if you need any iron or vitamin therapy to attain maximum strength and health. He will examine you internally, noting the condition of your cervix, the tone of the muscles around the vagina, and the size and position of your uterus.

He may prescribe special exercises to restore the tone of the vaginal muscles, if these are found to be weak. Such exercises consist essentially of drawing up the rectum—as though attempting to restrain an urge to move the bowels. This must be performed many times a day in order to strengthen the sling of muscles that supports the vagina, bladder, and rectum.

If your uterus is found to be "tipped," your obstetrician must decide whether to attempt replacing it. If he knows from previous examinations that your uterus is normally in

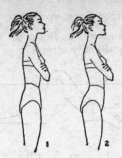

FIGURE G. Posture during Pregnancy

1. Proper way to carry your body during pregnancy: figure erect, shoulders up, back straight, stomach held in, chest up. Natural-childbirth advocates recommend that you consciously practice this proper method of posture to relieve the strain of carrying your baby as much as possible.
2. Incorrect posture during pregnancy: swaybacked, shoulders slumping, allowing abdomen to sag forward. This increases the strain of carrying weight of your growing baby.

this tipped position, he will probably not consider it useful to attempt to change it, since it will undoubtedly fall back to its former place. There is no special advantage to be gained from attempting to keep such a uterus forward.

The cervix frequently suffers laceration—even in the normal spontaneous birth. If neglected, this may lead to unpleasant discharges. It may be treated chemically or with the electric cautery.

Resuming sex activity. If laceration of the cervix or vagina has required treatment at the first visit to your obstetrician after delivery, the resumption of sexual relations may be further delayed. Otherwise, once this first checkup is completed you may feel free to indulge in all normal activities, including sex. Those whose beliefs permit may discuss birth control with the doctor at this time.

The first few times intercourse is attempted there may be some pain. Contraction of the scar, if there was an incision at delivery, causes a tightness of the vagina and a distinctly virginal feeling. It is advisable to use a lubricating jelly until this discomfort disappears.

A certain percentage of women will complain of discomfort

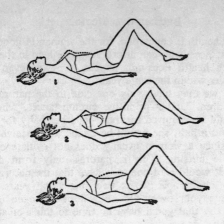

Childbirth Advocates

They urge women to practice this during pregnancy, feeling that its use during labor will ease the labor pains. Whenever a woman feels a pang coming on during labor, she is urged to concentrate on this breathing or "panting" exercise.

1 and 2. Panting through open mouth (otherwise known as "sternal breathing"). Dotted lines show how breastbone rises and lowers with this breathing exercise.

3. "Diaphragmatic" breathing during labor to ease the pangs. Dotted line shows how relaxed abdominal wall rises and lowers during this exercise.

FIGURE H. Breathing Exercise Recommended by Natural-

in their sexual relations for months after having a baby. It is usually found that this is not so much a physical result of delivery, but a psychological effect, due to the anxiety and fatigue which go with care of a baby. This causes a temporary loss of interest in sex. Without sexual excitement, the muscles about the vagina do not relax and intercourse is painful.

Reassurance and patience are the only treatment required.

Your next pregnancy. You will continue to make visits to your obstetrician until you are completely recovered and back to normal. One question then remains: How soon is it advisable to have your next baby?

As far as health is concerned, for the woman in good financial circumstances, who can afford adequate help in the home, the mother's health does not appear to suffer even if she has two babies within the same year.

Actually, we may have only one clue to the natural spacing of children. Under primitive circumstances, where the mother would be required to breast-feed her baby for a year to a year and a half, she would be unable to conceive during that time, since a woman usually does not ovulate or menstruate while nursing. This is nature's only form of contraception. It would lead one to believe that the natural interval between children is two to two and a half years.

For a time your every second will be so taken up with your new baby that you'll have no time to think of anything else. But then:

> *As diapers give way to training pants,*
> *And the dark of the night is for sleep;*
> *Be advised in advance, there's more than a chance,*
> *This book is a book you should keep.*

> *As training pants follow the diapers,*
> *And life holds a little more fun;*
> *Don't mutter that men are such vipers;*
> *Relax, and turn back to page one.*

Index

240   BECOMING A MOTHER